The

Obelisk

And other tales, wonderful and bizarre

by

David Lewis Paget

For my American Muse
who knows who she is....

Poetry by the same author:
Pen & Ink – the Complete Works 1968 - 2008
Timepieces – Poems Out of Time & Other Places
At Journey's End – Narrative Poems Vol. II
The Demon Horse on the Carousel – and Other Gothic Delights
Poems of Myth & Scare
The Devil on the Tree – and Other Poems of Dysfunction
Tales from the Magi
Taking Root
The Storm and the Tall Ship Pier
The Book on the Topmost Shelf
Tall Tales for Tired Times
Butterflies
The Widow of Martin Black
Goblin Dell
The Mind Catcher
The Angel of Lygon Street
The Season of the Witch
Smugglers Pie
My China
The Red Knight

ISBN – 978-0-646-97888-8

BARR BOOKS

Poetry Contents

Foreword

This, my sixteenth volume of narrative poems, is what you might call a mixed bag. If you bought this in a lolly shop, you would find the usual sickly pink sugary ones, the sour teddies, and the chocolate smoothies. But wriggling around the bottom of the bag would be some that defied description, black and glutinous, with names like dark dreams and shadowy freakshows. Unless you held on tightly these would seek to escape from the bag and go for your throat. They exist on the periphery of horrible, or skate along the landscape of myth. They contain characters not in control of their own destimy, and are most comfortable in dark rooms by dim reading lamps, where they can invade the reader's brain and create the most havoc. If you're not extra careful they will escape to your bedroom and hide beneath your pillow, ready to insinuate themselves into your dreams.

In a positive sense, I can say that each narrative is unique in its own way, having unravelled on high from some twisted skein of human experience, settling unnoticed in the imagination until brought to light by the scratch of a pen on paper. But don't expect normal, for normal is not to be found in these pages. These are twisted tales about twisted people living in twisted situations, and ruled by events outside their own control.

This collection finishes up with my 1400th poem, written since 1966. Even I find it hard to fathom how I've managed to write 1400 plots when there are only 6 known to literature. But as Americans would say: 'Go Figure!'

David Lewis Paget   October 2017

The Obelisk

Right at the top of the mountain
Stood an obelisk in stone,
It pointed up to the heavens
Was inscribed with a runic poem,
It wasn't known who had put it there
Or when, though it made no odds,
For men had seen it had always been
From the time of the ancient gods.

It had seemed to have strange properties
It changed, when the stone was wet,
Deep in the midst of a thunderstorm
It went from grey to jet,
The stone would glisten and glow at night
In a way that seemed most odd,
And when the lightning came forking down
Would act as a lightning rod.

It stood in a pleasant clearing
No tree would grow too near,
Though trees grew all up the mountainside,
I thought that fact was queer.
We'd take a picnic basket there
And settle on the slope,
Lie in the shade of the obelisk
Just me and my girlfriend, Hope.

And she would recline and rest there,
She was pleasing to the eye,
She looked like a Grecian Goddess
For her eyes would match the sky,

Her hair the colour of yellow straw,
She turned, and she sighed at me,
Then said, 'I feel I've been here before
In some ancient mystery.'

She couldn't explain just what she meant
So we lay awhile, and kissed,
Up on the sun drenched mountain top
In the shade of the obelisk,
Then she got restless and wandered up
To the face that held the runes,
And traced her fingers across the script
On that sunny afternoon.

I started up when I heard her scream
And I saw the arm and fist,
That slid on out of the solid stone
And seized her by the wrist,
The lettering of the runes lit up
And they glowed a scarlet red,
While I grabbed hold of her other arm,
Held onto her, in dread.

She couldn't manage to free herself
The hand held her so tight,
I strained and heaved, I could not believe,
But she turned pale, and white,
Her eyes went up in her head, then she
Fell fainting to the ground,
The hand still holding her by the wrist
But now there was no sound.

A shape rose out of her body there
Of mist, I couldn't hold,
And slid right into the solid stone,
It must have been her soul,
For then the hand, it had disappeared
And left an empty shell,
It left her body behind, but Hope,
I knew, had gone to hell.

She sits in a sanatorium
By the window, every day,
And looks unknowingly through the pane
While my pain won't go away.
I copied the rune and translated it
And it said, 'The God of Life,
Is trapped in stone in this Obelisk,
And he needs to find a wife…'

The Incubus

The day the devil came down to earth
And lodged in Katrina's heart,
It took me suddenly by surprise
When she shot his poisoned dart,
I'd known he was out to get me since
I'd got wised up to his tricks,
But I didn't think that he'd use my girl
To blow my world to bits.

She'd always been such a loving girl
With her pure and slothful eyes,
I didn't know that behind that smile
Was a cesspool full of lies,
He'd burrowed deep in her afterglow
And had twisted her inside,
I didn't know it was him not her,
For her purity had died.

The day she opened her mouth I saw
That her tongue was hard and black,
The words she uttered were never hers
But a blatant, harsh attack,
I sat there stunned for a moment with
My face as white as a sheet,
'Where on earth is that coming from,'
I said to her, 'my sweet?'

She said that she'd never loved me and
That love was just a crock,
She felt that she was above me, well,
I stared at her in shock,

She said she'd lain with another man
On just the night before,
I'd thought that I was a lover, but
She said he was so much more.

She pressed all my tender buttons and
She made me feel quite sick,
She knew how to disarray me and
Her poison acted quick,
I asked her if I had done something
To spawn this stream of stuff,
She said that I didn't need to,
Being me was quite enough.

I said that I'd better leave then, if
That's all that I meant to her,
She called me a craven coward, and
A crawling, slinking cur,
Her tongue rolled back and it blocked her throat
She began to gasp and choke,
So I reached inside and I grabbed her tongue
As she screamed in a long, high note.

The tongue came out like an evil snake
It was long, and black as ink,
It came away in my hand and left
A small one, that was pink,
It wriggled over the floor and I
Then stamped it into a pulp,
While Katrina drew a massive breath,
All she could do was gulp.

She couldn't remember a thing she'd said
So I said, it's up to us,
Whatever it was, that blackened tongue
Was the devil's incubus,
She cried and said that she loved me
It would be just as it was before,
But I look out for that incubus,
A seed from the devil's spore.

Sisterhood

She stared at him out of the paper
And he recognised her eyes,
He knew he'd seen them before, somewhere,
But her face was a different size,
There wasn't a dimple in the cheek
And her lips were rather thin,
It said that she was her sister, so
He sat, remembering.

The girl that he'd met in the nightclub
Who had stared across the room,
Their eyes had met in a brief vignette
And held, in the smoke-filled gloom,
They'd danced at the end of the evening
And he'd said he'd take her home,
The thought of a kiss from those ruby lips
Had driven his hands to roam.

She'd slapped his face, he remembered that,
But the rest was just a blur,
But now, from out of the newspaper
He was quite entranced by her,
He'd not read much of the article
For his reading skills were slight,
But he made his way to the same lane way
Where he'd held her sister tight.

The house was an old Victorian
With a gable above her room,
He saw the light on that winter's night
That lit the surrounding gloom,

13

Her shape appeared in the window frame
As she stared down at the ground,
He thought he knew she would want him to
So he stayed, and hung around.

He stood right under a lamp post and
Was lit by a single beam,
While she stared down from the window, and
He knew that he'd been seen,
The door had creaked as it opened up
And she walked into the lane,
While he, now full of bravado, said,
'It's nice to see you, Jane.'

She paused, just inches away from him,
And she said, 'my name is Joan,
You must have been with my sister
On that night she was alone.'
He looked confused, and then quite amused
At the harshness in her voice,
Then said, 'I'd rather have been with you
If I'd only had the choice.'

'I knew that you would come back one day,
Though I knew you'd take your time,
The killer always comes back, they say
To the place they did the crime.'
He stared right into her eyes just then
And he saw the eyes of Jane,
His fingers wrapping around her neck
As she stared at him in pain.

'She really shouldn't have slapped my face,'
He said, 'it wasn't right,
All that I did was touch her breast
Before a kiss goodnight.'
But then he staggered in shock and pain
To feel what her sister did,
As the kitchen knife slid in between
His first and his second rib.

Castle Krake

I'd always wanted a castle, so
I bought one in the Spring.
It wasn't much of a castle,
Overgrown with everything,
Ivy covered the castle walls
There were trees on the battlements,
And bushes grew in the courtyard,
But I bought the place for cents.

They said it hadn't been lived in since
The days of Charles the First,
And Cromwell's troops had reduced it with
A mighty cannon burst.
The gatehouse lay in a ruin where
The Army stormed inside,
And hunted down the defenders there
Who, to a man, had died.

The women, hid in the kitchen there,
Eventually were caught,
The older ones had their throats cut,
But the young ones kept for sport,

And Lady May in her boudoir, she
Was seized by a Captain Clyne,
Who dragged her out by her hair, and said,
'Not this one, she'll be mine!'

He ripped and clawed at her bodice till
She was exposed to view,
She screamed that he was an animal,
'I'll never lie with you!'
He laughed and shackled her hands and feet
And he took his wicked will,
She sobbed to say he would have to pay
For the virgin blood he'd spilled.

'I'll hunt you down like the cur you are,
I will follow you through time,
My downline will seek yours to kill
For vengeance will be mine.'
He laughed, but fate, it had lain in wait
When a pile of shattered stones,
That hung so perilous by the gate
Had crushed his evil bones.

I took delight in the story when
I purchased this ancient pile,
And sat in the ancient boudoir where
I was pensive, for a while.
So this was the place that it happened,
Just above a flagstoned stair,
The rape of an ancient beauty, that
Had seeped in the walls in there.

It took some months to clean up the place
Ripping out each bush and tree,
Till Castle Krake was taking shape
And making a home for me.
I slept up there in the boudoir
During those long, cold winter nights,
With only a blazing brazier
And a sputtering torch for lights.

One night I heard a commotion, it
Was down by the Castle Keep,
A sound, a clashing of soldiers,
I woke from a shallow sleep.
And then was a woman sobbing,
It echoed within the walls,
For soon she screamed, 'I will hunt you down,'
As I lay there, quite appalled.

Since then, there have been accidents
Of masonry falls and such,
The brazier set my bed alight
I escaped by just a touch,
It's all to do with that Captain Clyne
And the curse of Lady May,
For Captain Clyne's in my mother's line
So I don't feel safe today.

The Day the Poet Died

The trees are dry, have a withered look
And the wheat has gone to seed,
The skies are grey on a summer's day
And the river's filled with weed,
The brook that babbled is sad and still
And the sea lies flat beside,
A lonely shore that had offered more
Till the day the poet died.

Gone is the sound of merriment
And the party jokes fall flat,
The folk just wander aimlessly
As they turn to this and that,
The traffic's down to a sullen crawl
As the lights turn red beside,
And silence falls like a dreadful pall
Since the day the poet died.

The colours leach from the neon signs
And they turn a pavement grey,
There is no yellow or green chartreuse
To be seen since that dreadful day,
The liquor's flat as a pieman's hat
And you can't get drunk, they sighed,
The children say they will run away
Now they know that the poet died.

And love has curdled in every heart
It was captured in his verse,
The sweet young bride has been left outside
Where no bells ring, which is worse,

The Moon at night is without its light
That it once would shine outside,
And lovers look for its beam in vain
Since the day that the poet died.

There is no poetry left in life
That was back in another time,
When the poet cursed as he wove his verse
And he sprinkled it well with rhyme,
But it's sad to say, now he's gone away
We must learn to feel inside,
And colour our world a different way,
Now that the poet's died.

So Many Years

So many years have passed us by,
So many great events,
Sometimes I smile, or sit and cry
At some of the incidents.
Those were the days when we were young
And love an affair of the heart,
But love came and went, remained unsung
By tearing us all apart.

All we have left are photographs
And many are stained by tears,
Where did they go, those joyous laughs
Echoing through the years?

The love that was made has disappeared
Swallowed by Father Time,
And even the children that we reared
Have left for another clime.

Where are the friends that brought us joy,
Where is the merriment,
Where are the girls who acted coy
We thought they were heaven sent.
Scattered to where the four winds blow
And lost to each chilling breeze,
A fading memory, fluttering by
Like the scatter of Autumn leaves.

And those we lost loom large in the dark
When we lie on the verge of sleep,
They flit on by like the vital spark
They lost, when the mere was deep,
For those that died will never return,
They left on the final bus,
That grim old hearse, pulled by a horse
That now is waiting for us.

The Tunnel

The house dated back to the Tudors,
Half timbered, in need of repair,
They offered it me for a peppercorn rent
If I'd do some work on it there.
Right next to it stood the Catholic Church,
All pillars and deep seated vaults,
I thought I could make it a comfortable lair
Despite its old timbers and faults.

But Kathy was not so enamoured,
She said that she'd rather a flat,
'There's dry rot and beetles,' she stammered,
'So what will you do about that?'
'I'll think about that in the morning,
For now you'll just have to be brave,
You'll love that old bed, and its awning,
And think of the money we'll save.'

We got settled in and explored it,
The wainscoting seemed to be fine,
With three rooms upstairs, and an attic,
I seized on that, told her, 'It's mine!'
She wouldn't come down to the cellar,
'It's too dark and creepy for me.'
I thought it would do for a storeroom,
It had its own hearth, and chimney.

One day I had leant on the mantle
When something had moved in the wall,
A bookshelf slid back near a candle,
Revealing an ancient priest hole,

But way beyond that was a tunnel
The led all the way to a crypt,
So this was their ancient escape route
For anything termed Catholic.

I thought I would wait to explore it
Till Kathy would like to come too,
But she had just shivered, ignored it,
And said, 'you just do what you do.'
I couldn't contain my excitement
As into that tunnel I went,
Imagining priests that had used it,
To burn at the stake, or repent.

Then halfway along in an alcove
I flashed the light, looking in there,
And there was a man in some red robes,
He sat, sprawling back in a chair,
And there on his skull was a mitre
That headdress for bishops of old,
And down by his side was a crozier,
All glittering, fashioned in gold.

But lying between his skeletal feet
Was a sight that I couldn't absorb,
I felt at a loss, on top was a cross
On a gold and magnificent orb,
Caught short in his flight from the protestant's might
He was stealing these treasures away,
In hopes that the realm of England returned
To the one true religion one day.

I picked up the crozier, picked up the orb
And I took them from where he had fled,
I didn't tell Kathy, but thought it was best,
So I hid them both under our bed.
That night we heard chanting, a hymn in the dark
That had Kathy awake and in tears,
While I could see phantoms surrounding our bed
Giving form to a host of my fears.

There was an abomination of monks
That were filling the room from the stairs,
And chief among them was a bishop who stood
At the base of the bed, and just glared.
I leapt out of bed and recovered the orb,
And I handed the crozier to him,
He gave a faint smile, and then in a while
He was gone like a ghost cherubim.

I never went back to that tunnel again,
To tell you the truth, I was scared,
I knew that a fortune was hidden within
But to go back again, never dared.
I'm hoping that bishop has saved me a place
In a heaven for those who are saved,
So I can tell no-one where he lies in grace,
That knowledge I'll take to my grave.

The Pet Octopus

While wandering on a local beach
Half buried in weed and sand,
The sparkle of something caught my eye
The shape of an old tin can.
I kicked it loose from entangling weed
And saw there was something within,
A colourful creature there indeed,
An octopus in a tin.

I thought it cute so I took it home
To put in the garden pond,
Then added salt for a briny mix
So it wouldn't think to abscond.
It swam on out of the tin to feed
And seized on a goldfish there,
I said to Diane, 'He has a need,'
While she just tore at her hair.

'What were you thinking?' Diane said,
'It'll eat all the fish we've got,'
'They're only a couple of bucks,' I said,
'I'll get some more at the shop.'
He settled right in, our strangest pet,
And cost us to feed the least,
I said that I'd name the tinker, 'Jet',
Diane just called him 'The Beast'.

He started to grow, outgrew his can,
So settled down in the depths,
He couldn't be seen for thick pondweed,
Diane said,'It's for the best.'

The dog would bark when The Beast came up,
Would stand there, wagging his tail.
We loved that dog, though barely a pup,
Then Diane began to wail.

'It's eaten the effing dog,' she said,
Her language was more than coarse,
And Rin-Tin-Tin in the pond was skin,
She said, 'Keep it away from my horse!'
I poked around in the pool for him
Just trying to make him rise,
He bit the end of my pole clean off,
He must have grown to a size.

She said I had to stop feeding him
But that only made it worse,
He looked for food, and he got the cat
As it chased a couple of birds.
Diane was walking down by the pond
When I suddenly heard her scream,
A tentacle wrapped around her leg
It looked like a nightmare scene.

I tried my best to peel it away
The octopus was too strong,
Diane went struggling over the edge
And fell right into the pond,
It took her down to the lower depths
And ate her, clean to the bone,
I tell this tale, so you won't forget,
Don't take an octopus home.

A Gypsy Tease

Down in the lower farmer's field
Was an old style gypsy camp,
The wagons drawn in a circle,
Each one lit with a paraffin lamp,
And there in the centre of them all
A bonfire burned all night,
The flames would leap and the shadows creep
In a sort of mystic flight.

I'd watch from a grove of elder trees
As the gypsies sang and danced,
The girls would swirl their skirts to tease
As they whirled around and pranced,
Their arms were covered with bangles and
Their fingers, bright with rings,
Would flash at night in the firelight
As the shadows gave them wings.

Most of the girls were young, but there
Was a single one, my age,
Who danced with grace in an open space
She was on a separate page,
Her hair was black as a raven, and
Her lips the colour of blood,
My heart was stilled, it was almost chilled
By the view, from where I stood.

Her eyes were dark, they were almost black
Her hue the colour of sand,
I thought that it might be natural
Or perhaps her skin was tanned,

But as if she read my thoughts one day
She had twirled her dress up high,
And that same bright golden colour rose,
Ran up each fabulous thigh.

Then I saw her at the village fair
In the Fortune Teller's booth,
I paid my money to go in there
And I found her name was Ruth,
She gazed deep into her crystal ball
And I saw her start to flush,
I said, 'and what can you see in there,'
When the flush became a blush.

'I've never seen such a thing before,'
She said, her eyes cast low,
'I cannot tell you your fortune now,
So sir, you will have to go.'
She rose and pushed me out of the tent
But I gazed into her eyes,
And saw the future of my intent
In her look of blank surprise.

I went again and she read the cards
Wouldn't touch the crystal ball,
She said, 'there's something very strange
In the way the cards will fall.'
I blurted out that I loved her hair
That I'd watched her from afar,
She smiled and said, I would turn her head,
'I had wondered who you are.'

27

Then we stood together in that booth
And I stole a single kiss,
She fell into my arms, and cried,
'I could not imagine this.
But the crystal ball, it never lies
And the cards have joined us too,'
She gave me one of her gypsy sighs,
Said, 'What are we going to do?'

In Search of...

The woman to grace my garden would
Have generous hips and thighs,
Long curling hair and a playful stare
A come hither look in her eyes,
A dimple set in a smiling cheek
And lips that would sometimes pout,
She'd move with grace at a steady pace
And her love would knock me out.

We'd meet at noon by the garden seat
In the shade of an apple tree,
With a plate of scones, and jam and cream
That her hands laid out for me,
We'd read a book in that shady nook
As we ate, drank lemonade,
I'd hold her hand in that magic land
And smile, at the game we played.

Then when the day had begun to cool
I'd wrap her up in a shawl,
Our summer days would begin to fade,
We'd still be there in the Fall,
Our talk would cover a thousand things
But we'd marvel most at life,
That fate had brought us together, she'd
Be proud to be called my wife.

My thoughts still stand in that happy land
As I sit alone in this,
And wonder where she may be out there
For a life, so full of bliss,

I sit and wait by the garden gate
For her form to pass on by,
Our eyes may meet in this dismal street
Until then, I'll sit and sigh.

Two Brothers

They'd built too close to the cliffside edge
And the winters grew so cold,
The ocean seemed to be rising with
The waves, as in they rolled,
They tore away the base of the cliff
And swept it out to sea,
The house was poised on the cliffside edge
And would soon be history.

Two brothers lived in the fated house
That had once comprised of three,
For one of the brothers had a wife
Who was called Penelope,
But something funny was going on
The folks around there said,
For Penny was always seen with John
But had been the wife of Fred.

They both had courted the girl before
And each had bought a ring,
Then asked Penelope could she choose
Between them, there's the thing,
She told the brothers she loved them both,
The choice was hard, she said,
'A half of me would marry with John,
But I have to go with Fred.'

The rumours started around the town
That she had the best of two,
She'd sleep for half a week with Fred
And the rest, with you know who.
They'd say that voices were raised in there
It wasn't going well,
What should have been a heaven on earth
Would seem some kind of hell.

For just on a year she went to town
And shopped just like the rest,
She smiled that bright Penelope smile
Was always nicely dressed,
But then she stopped, and she wasn't seen
As the brothers did the shop,
Then they would glower at everything
And they wouldn't talk, or stop.

But still the sound of their voices raised
Would echo from that house,
Til Fred stopped going around with John,
There was no sign of his spouse,
The storm that came at the midnight hour
Then washed away the cliff,
The house plunged into the water and
The rumours said, 'What if?'

The house was shattered as in it plunged
Each piece was washed away,
And morning had seen the strangest sight,
A coffin, out in the bay,

The rescue boat had dragged it in
And dumped it up on the shore,
Along with a drenched Penelope
So they wondered, more and more.

They found a body, washed on the beach,
It was hard to recognise,
They asked Penelope could she view them
Once she'd dried her eyes,
They opened the coffin for her first
And in there lay her Fred,
His throat was bloody and torn apart
And Penelope bowed her head.

'I got so sick of the arguments,
It was like being wed to two,
They raved and ranted most every day
I didn't know what to do.'
'You say John murdered his brother then?'
But the police were being kind,
Penelope shook her head, and said,
'I suddenly changed my mind.'

Stored in the Heart

I had no idea of who she was,
But knew she appealed to me,
All that I knew, her name was Roz,
So I wove her history.
Imagination's a marvellous thing
But that doesn't make it real,
I thought I could make the whole thing up
But I only judge by feel.

I had her grow in a miserable home
Where no-one could understand,
A feckless mother and drunken Dad
With no-one to hold her hand.
She'd come to life when she left that home,
Left everything else behind,
And if she wasn't together yet,
Then everyone else was blind.

I loved the way that her hair curled down
To sit at the nape of her neck,
I loved that serious air she had
To hold everyone in check.
I didn't know if she noticed me
She never gave me a look,
Whenever she passed my desk, I sat
And buried my head in a book.

We used the stationery storeroom there,
It was big enough for two,
I walked on in and I locked the door,
Said, 'I've been looking at you.'

She seemed surprised and had startled eyes
When I drew her close for a kiss,
But she raised her lips and she moved her hips,
So it didn't seem too remiss.

She met me down at the local pub
To discuss the feelings she had,
'It's not that I didn't enjoy the kiss,
I don't want you feeling bad.
But I have a guy and he's awful shy,
So don't tell what happened today,
Some things are sacred, stored in the heart,'
And then she had walked away.

Of Comets and Bats

It's four o'clock, and I'm wide awake
Too early for pre-dawn light,
Thinking about the night before
And the reason we had that fight.
You never listen to what I say,
And it makes me feel so mad,
Whenever you get that cauldron out,
Your recipes smell so bad.

I'd told you there was a comet due
And I even wore my hat,
Trying to mask that smell of stew
When you crucified the bat,
You kept on adding ingredients
When I told you, 'that will do.'
I used the peg when the dead dog's leg
Went flying into the stew.

I knew when you wore your pointy hat
And your cape with the flowing hood,
Whatever you cooked up there last night
Was something you never should.
You always try to get back at me
When I talk about the stars,
And say, 'So what,' that the art you've got
You picked up yourself, on Mars.

I knew the spell that you wove last night
Was something that wasn't good,
You even opened our one skylight
To draw in the neighbourhood.

Not everyone wants a witches curse
To dangle from every tree,
But you don't care, do it for a dare,
But mainly to get at me.

I saw the trail in the midnight sky
And tried to put out the fire,
But you were fey, and pushed me away,
Then tossed on a bicycle tyre.
I ran out into the garden then,
Into the dark of night,
And watched as the tiny comet came
To crash through our own skylight.

There's nothing that you can blame me for
It's not as if you forgot,
It flew on in to your spell of sin
And dropped in your cooking pot,
It flashed and blazed and sizzled in there
And now, you are looking weird,
You wore your recipe in your hair,
But where did you get that beard?

Death Wish

She said she wanted to kill herself
Since her life was empty now,
I couldn't figure it out myself
And called her a silly cow,
'Your Barry isn't the only one,
There's lots more fish in the sea,'
But she just said that her love was dead,
'He's the only one for me.'

I wanted to tell her nonsense, that
She should take stock of me,
I'd be her friend to the living end,
I'd known her since she was three.
I told her once that I'd marry her
When we both were eight or nine,
But what I'd said must have left her head,
Lost in the mists of time.

It's hard to be friends and lovers, both,
Though our friendship was sublime,
The love was buried in friendship, was
Invisible, undermined,
She missed the sparkle in both my eyes
Whenever she came my way,
I always wanted to tell her but
I didn't have words to say.

Then Barry captured her from me when
She'd just turned seventeen,
He must have had something on me, though
I'd not see what she'd seen.

I should have known there was something on
When she turned from me out there,
And he came wandering in one day
With ribbons for her hair.

And that was the end of hopes and dreams
That I'd held from childhood days,
For Barry was full of exciting schemes,
She was thrilled in many ways,
She'd say, 'I've never known anyone
Who excites me like he can,'
And from then on she was truly gone
And refused to hold my hand.

It only lasted a year or two
Until Barry lost the plot,
He found more interesting girls out there
Who'd got what she hadn't got.
'I don't know what has gone wrong with us,'
She cried, all out of breath,
'I won't be sticking around, I know,
This life now seems like death.'

We went out walking along the cliff
She strayed too close to the top,
And said, 'I think to myself, what if
I should suddenly drop,'
I pulled her down as she stepped too close
And pinned her onto to the ground,
'What would my life be worth if you
Were suddenly not around?'

She looked at me in amazement as
She suddenly saw me there,
I kissed her once and she kissed me back,
'I didn't know that you'd care.'
'You fool, I've loved you forever, but
I didn't think it would show,'
'My life is suddenly full,' she said,
'But I just needed to know.'

The Visitor

He drove on up to the Nursing Home
For the first time in a year,
He needed to get some papers signed
So he sought his mother there,
The matron pointed him to her room
With a wave of a careless hand,
But sitting next to his mother's bed
Was the figure of a man.

'So what the hell is he doing here?'
Said the son, in a burst of rage,
'He has no right to be visiting,
To be here, at any stage,
They've been divorced for eleven years
And I thought he'd gone for good,
He'll just reduce my mother to tears,
You should ban him, yes, you should.'

The matron halted outside the door
And she went to hold him back,
She said, 'Oh yes, I know you now,
You're the son they all call Jack.
She probably doesn't remember you,
But you see, he comes each noon,
He sits and chats, and he holds her hand
And he feeds her with a spoon.'

'Her mind has wandered away, you see,'
Said the matron, with a smile,
'She's somewhere back where she used to be,
But you, it has been a while.

There's not the staff to attend to her,
If I institute your ban,
You'll come each day, and you'll fend for her?'
He said, 'I don't think I can.'

He watched them both from outside the door
And he saw his mother smile,
The man he'd known as a stepfather
Was as gentle as a child,
He stood outside and he caught her eye
But she gave no sign she knew,
He bowed his head and the matron said,
'I would call that love, would you?'

He put the papers away, he knew
That she wasn't fit to sign,
Then turned to go as he said, 'You know,
I'll come at a better time.'
The matron ushered him to the door
And she said, 'We'll see you, Jack,'
But deep inside was a truth that cried
He'd never be coming back.

The Painting

The painting sat in an old junk shop
At the far end of The Strand,
It caught my eye and it made me stop
Though the subject wasn't grand.
A woman stood in a window frame
And she stared out at the street,
The pavement there was of cobblestones
And the whole thing was, well, neat!

The basic thing that had caught my eye
Was the woman's face, I know,
I didn't think she had sat for it
But it looked like Billie Jo.
The likeness there was remarkable
In the lips, that sullen pout,
The hooded eyes that had looked so wise,
Overall, it knocked me out.

I bought the painting and took it home
And I showed my Billie Jo,
She couldn't believe the likeness, and
I said, 'I told you so.'
'You're sure that you didn't sit for this,
I find it rather strange?'
The look on her face said something else,
Like guilt, but rearranged.

'I don't want to talk about the thing,
You shouldn't have brought it home,
The look of that woman's creepy,
I'd have left it well alone.'

'It's almost as if you have a twin,'
I said to Billie Jo,
'There may be some things about you, girl,
You don't want me to know.'

She shrugged, and she walked away just then
So I hung it on the wall,
She made me pull it down and hang it
Somewhere in the hall,
She didn't care just where, she said
But she didn't want to see,
The face of that strange woman, she said,
'Looking back at me.'

The footsteps came on that very night
And they padded in the hall,
We woke and we lay awake in dread
And Billie began to bawl.
'She's come, I know that she's come for me,
When I thought I'd put her down,
The day that she rode that coal black hearse,
And was buried in the ground.'

I said that she'd best come clean with me
And she told about her twin,
'I didn't tell you before, because she
Frightened me out of my skin.
She used to say that she hated me
And would somehow bring me harm,
I caught her poisoning fizzy drinks
When we lived down on the farm.'

'We had a fight in the cattle yard
That was one of her designs,
She kicked at me and she fell back hard,
Impaled on the baler tines.
She coughed up blood and she looked at me
And she spat, with her final breath,
'You'll not escape, I'll open the gates
Of hell, to do you death.''

'She must have posed for that picture
In the week before she died,
And you have brought her on home to me,
I could swear that the picture sighed.'
I took it away the following day
And I burnt it in the well,
As the fire devoured the woman's face,
It shrieked, from the gates of hell.

Another World

Walking among the Autumn leaves
On a cold and blustery day,
Between an avenue of trees
As the daylight passed away,
The shadows lengthened across my path
And my way was hit or miss,
As a sudden wind would seem to blend
My other world, with this.

A world where nothing would make much sense
I'd lost it all, I knew,
Where day was night when it should be bright
And it left me, looking for you,
A world of shadows and woods and streams
Where there'd been a town before,
And the sea crept in where it might have been
For a million years or more.

While creatures high in the treetops there
Reflected their blinking eyes,
From a sudden ray at the close of day,
Just as the Moon would rise,
It was such an alien place to be
It was grim, and chill, and old,
As I wandered by an ancient sea
In a dark place of the soul.

I remembered how you had said to me
On the last day that we'd met,
How I would rue the loss of you
In a wasteland of regret.

And I had laughed as I slammed the door
To return the way I came,
Not thinking that I would miss you too,
But the end result was pain.

While you remained in the hospital
And stared with your sunken eyes,
I couldn't bear that I'd put you there
With my lack of care, and my lies.
The doctor said you were almost dead
With your heart split open wide,
It's only now, and it must be said,
That it wasn't you that died.

An Affair of the Heart

They moved right in to the house next door
To our great regret, and pain,
It sounded as if they'd gone to war
Or the two were quite insane,
We should have kept right away from them
But did the neighbourly bit,
Went over and introduced ourselves
And watched them hiss and spit.

They couldn't seem to control themselves
Not even in front of us,
If Jill had spoken to me like that
I'd have pushed her under a bus.
And if I'd shown her the same contempt
That Ray had shown to Liz,
She'd fly at me with a kitchen knife
Because that's the way it is.

We left them there and we went back home
But appalled, with eyebrows raised,
'Thank god that we're not like them,' we said,
Our relationship we praised,
They never stopped, we could hear them both
As they each tore each apart,
'Why do they stay together that way?
It's not an affair of the heart.'

We found that we had to go to them
On a crisp, September night,
They asked us both to adjudicate
After a terrible fight,

So I sat down with Liz, and Jill
Sat listening to Ray,
And after we got back home again
We had different things to say.

'That Ray is the monster of the two,'
I said, 'for he's always wrong,'
'That Liz is a shrew, I'm telling you,'
Said Jill as she sang his song.
We couldn't agree on anything,
We even began to fight,
We had to agree to disagree
As I slept on the couch that night.

Then Jill took to walking in the park
With Ray as the nights wore on,
While I sat with Liz, here, in the dark,
And hugged her, while they were gone,
But never a word amiss was said,
You wouldn't believe it true,
'For Ray is a perfect gentleman,'
Said Jill, 'and nicer than you.'

'Well, Liz would have been my heart's desire,
If I'd only met her first,'
The terrible jibes were steel and fire,
It seemed that we both were cursed,
And then came the day Jill ran away,
With Ray, and I slept with Liz,
I said that I'd love her every day
For that is the way it is.

A year went by and I saw Jill cry
When we met at night in the dark,
And I was miserable too, I sighed,
To Jill in the midnight park,
'What happened to our relationship,
We seem to have come off worse,'
'They're both as bad as each other, Jill,
Meeting them was a curse.'

But there was never a going back
To capture what we had lost,
We'd been the tools of a pair of fools
And now were paying the cost,
For Liz flings terrible barbs at me
While Ray tears Jill apart,
We pay the price, and it isn't nice,
It's not an affair of the heart.

The Steamship Southern Star

My friend signed on to a coastal ship
His name, John Escobar,
He said, for only a week long trip
On the Steamship Southern Star.
While I worked out of the office of
The Southern Shipping Line,
To keep in touch with our fleet of ships,
But the Southern Star was mine.

They said that ship was a special case
It was fitted out so well,
They joked of equipment so refined
It could sail clear through to hell.
I'd noticed bulges down on the hull
But under the waterline,
They told me to keep an eye on it
When they said that it was mine.

It sailed on out of Ascension Bay
When the tide was running high,
The motor gave out a whisper like
The sound of a woman's sigh,
It wasn't supposed to leave the coast
But it went far out to sea,
And kept in touch with the dit-dit-dit
Of John on the morse code key.

He tapped a message out every hour
And I let him know I knew,
The ship was sailing way off its course
And lost to the coastal view,

He said the Captain was acting strange
He was locked up by the wheel,
That all the maps had been rearranged
And that something wasn't real.

At midnight there was a message came
To me in a darkened room,
It said, 'I don't know what's going on
But we just sailed past the Moon.'
I sent, 'Just lay off the Bourbon, John,
If this is John Escobar,'
And he replied that the Captain died,
'And I don't know where we are.'

He sent more messages on the hour
And they seemed to grow apace,
By midday out on the second day,
'We're somewhere out in space.'
I didn't know if he'd gone berserk
But we'd lost the Southern Star,
It disappeared, and the thing was weird,
When I lost John Escobar.

The messages gradually petered out
So I don't know if he lied,
He said some things about Saturn's rings
And then the battery died.
I lost my job at the shipping line
For they put it down to me,
They said, 'your ship was the Southern Star,
And you've lost the thing at sea.'

The Wheels of Time

The day was grey when it came my way
With a clatter of wheels and hooves,
Echoing off the cobblestones
And under the red tile roofs,
The rain was glistening in the road
And I was confused at first,
For what I'd thought was a coach and four
Went by as a horse drawn hearse.

The horse went stepping by, high and proud
With a coat like shining mail,
And ostrich plumes adorned its harness
Right down to its plaited tail.
Then in the hearse, a polished coffin
With silver plate inscribed,
The name of him, who encased within
Had clutched at his heart, and died.

I watched the hearse as it rolled away
And thought that it could be me,
When one day off in a future time
I departed my history,
The wheels had creaked like a ticking clock
Or a dripping tap, each turn,
Rolling along to the day we stopped,
Went home in a funeral urn.

The months slipped by with barely a sigh
Till I saw that hearse again,
It passed my way when the day was grey
And the clouds had threatened rain.

I read the name on the silver plate
As the hearse had passed on by,
And held my breath in the face of death
For I certainly knew that guy.

We'd been together at school back when
Though he was younger than me,
He'd been successful in all he'd done
And married Penelope.
The only woman I'd ever loved
But he'd snatched her heart away,
And now she plodded behind the hearse
Looking faded, old and grey.

Her eyes met mine and a bitter smile
Had flickered around her eyes,
I hadn't seen her for years, and yet
Her look had the look of surprise.
I never saw her again until
She passed me by in the hearse,
Her name engraved on the silver plate,
I thought I was being cursed.

So now I wait by the garden gate
For the clatter of wheels and hooves,
Whenever the day is clouded and grey
And the sound echoes off the roofs.
All I can hear are the wheels of time
That pass like a ticking clock,
And wait for the hearse to halt outside,
Whether I know it, or not.

The Nightmare

She thought that she woke in the morning
To a world that was filled with dread,
Though nothing was changed, or rearranged
Her lover was surely dead.
He'd gone to drive in a shady lane
And said he'd be back by three,
A phone call brought her a wealth of pain,
His car crashed into a tree.

And all the lights in the world went out
For even the sun was dim,
Her love was grey, for a day away
Her life had revolved round him.
Never again would she see him smile,
Or feel the thrill of his touch,
Or roll and play in the barnyard hay
When she cried and sighed, 'Too much!'

But there in the darkness of her room
His phantom seemed to appear,
His face showed care as he stroked her hair,
'You know that I love you, dear.'
Her tears were like a river that flows
As she tossed and turned in the gloom,
'I never thought you would leave me here
To seek your rest in a tomb.'

And then she heard the jangle of keys
As she woke, and her eyes were wide,
He said, 'I thought I would let you sleep
While I went out for a ride.'

She leapt on him and she pulled him down
To the warm, soft quilt on the bed,
'The only ride you can take, is me,
My God! I dreamt you were dead!'

Suspicion

I heard the ring of the ambulance
As it barrelled down from E,
But wasn't really awake, so didn't
Know that it came for me.
They had me strapped on a stretcher
In the twinkling of an eye,
And only when we arrived, did I
Believe I was going to die.

The pain had been unrelenting since
I'd eaten the evening meal,
It started up in my shoulder, and
My hands, I couldn't feel,
I felt my head become groggy, till
I finally passed out,
It must have been when I hit the floor
That I heard your sudden shout.

They said it must be a heart attack
So they'd have to run a test,
But while I lay in the hospital
I'd better get some rest.
I kept on coming and going while
The questions filled my head,
I wondered if I'd been poisoned,
Did you really want me dead?

I'd thought that it tasted funny, at
The time, as I said to you,
The meat had had a consistency
As if it was cooked in glue,
And then some of those vegetables
I couldn't recognise,
You said I'd not know the difference
Between casseroles and pies.

And then, it must be about the time
That my forehead became damp,
You said whatever I knew of food
You could write on a postage stamp,
But you had been acting strangely since
That boarder came to stay,
Spending your time in drinking wine
That he'd brought from Bordelais.

I knew to look for the danger signs
In your long retreat from me,
I knew at once that he had designs
When his hand had touched your knee,
And every time that I left you two
Alone on a sultry day,
I had to wonder what you would do
To while the time away.

Your friend, Margot, has visited me
Alone in my hospital bed,
She said you were picking mushrooms,
Which has left my mind in dread.

She always seems to have favoured me,
And she sat and held my hand,
She said I shouldn't have married you,
This is what you would have planned.

My mind was full of suspicion when
You came to visit me,
But you had cried, said I almost died,
And that brought you misery.
'You know that I've always loved you,
But that love has brought me pain,
Whenever you look at Margot, it's
Like losing you again.'

I asked her about the boarder and
She said that he'd gone before,
'I only ever played up to him
To make you want me more.'
We're both a prey to suspicions
And the heartache that they lend,
We're over that, and we made a pact,
Our love is on the mend.

Nobody's Girl

The waves came crashing in from the sea
We were caught on a spit of land,
With no way back, not one I could see,
I reached and I held her hand.
'I've never seen the breakers so high,'
She cried, in a fit of fear,
'You must have known, it's hard to deny,
So why did you bring me here?'

'I brought you for a moment of truth,
A moment for you and I,
There's only you, and me and the sea,
This spit of land and the sky.
We never manage to be alone,
There's always somebody near,
And every time I open my mouth
There's somebody else to hear.'

The spray was drenching her beautiful hair,
And running into her eyes,
Her make-up running most everywhere,
It gave her a look of surprise.
'You might have picked a quieter spot,
We still could have been alone,
You never said what you wanted, or not.'
'I needed you on your own.'

'I needed to tell you that I'm in love,
Have been since the day we met,
But you've hung out with Derek, the drone,
I hoped that you'd leave him yet.'

'He's just a friend, I told you before,
He's easy to be around,
You do go on! He isn't my love,
You cover the same old ground.'

I took the ring from my sodden shirt
And held it for her to see,
'I'd like you to take this diamond ring,
And say you belong to me.'
'I only belong to myself,' she said,
'I'm nobody's girl in the end,
But if I put on your diamond ring,
I may just give you a lend.'

The breakers crashed, like a waterspout,
And washed us both off the spit,
We laughed so much as we flailed about,
Trying to swim through it.
We headed in to the distant beach
Together, and that was the thing,
For when we got to the sandy breach
I saw she was wearing the ring.

The Wench

He sat at the railway station in
The hopes of a passing train,
There hadn't been one for hours, while he
Was sheltering from the rain,
While over the opposite platform, sat
And sprawled on a wooden bench,
A sight to gladden a jaundiced eye,
A typical old-time wench.

For wenches were few and far between
In that post-industrial time,
As everyone wore both slacks and jeans,
And nothing to tease the mind,
But not this wench on the wooden bench
For she wore a floral dress,
A petticoat that was made of rope
That rose to her knees, no less.

And could those have been real stockings like
They'd been when he was a lad,
With straightened seams to the land of dreams
From calf to the thigh, well clad,
It put him in mind of the garter belts
That she'd have to wear, no doubt,
He'd seen in his teenage magazines
When he was a gadabout.

She rose and walked up the platform and
She gave her brolly a whirl,
And then he noticed her bodice with
Its buttons, mother of pearl,

Her hair was combed in a bouffant, piled
Up high in an auburn wave,
And dangling from her delicate ears
Were miniature rings of jade.

Two trains pulled into the station,
One each side and they climbed aboard,
Their windows were facing each other,
He faced back, while she faced forward,
Then just for a moment he smiled at her
And she smiled back from her bench,
As he muttered to her six silent words:
'By God! You're a beautiful wench!'

At Numero 69

They say it's been empty for quite some time,
But I've seen a flickering torch,
Late at night when the moon is bright
The light is red on the porch.
And shadows move by the hedgerows there
Like spectres that flit in the night,
The door will creak as the seekers seek,
While the blinds are pulled down tight.

And something creaks where the attic peaks
It could be a number of things,
A flutter of leaves, the wind in the eaves
Or the sound of some old bed springs.
The neighbours hide and they stay inside
When the Moon comes up on the rise,
They say no way can the children play,
It would be a blot on their eyes.

For Elspeth comes as the sun goes down
In a skirt as short as can be,
With fishnet tights in both blacks and whites,
They say she's brewing the tea.
Perhaps they're playing Canasta there
Or playing for poker chips,
They may be dancing the night away,
She sure has a dancer's hips.

Whatever it is they do in there
I'll have to go in to find,
The state of play that they do each day
At Numero sixty-nine.
I'll stay nonplussed till I get it sussed,
I wonder what it could be?
It's just my luck, if I go to look,
I'll catch her brewing the tea.

Nothing Gained

Wherever I go, I see her face
Reflected in streets and malls,
Wherever I track, in looking back
She's hiding behind stone walls,
I never manage to pin her down
I turn around and she's gone,
I don't know why she's following me
I ought to be moving on.

That isn't the way it always was
I'd see her down by the lake,
She'd sit on a bench beneath a tree,
While feeding the ducks and drake,
And I would sit on a nearby bench
And take in her golden hair,
Our eyes would meet, but very discreet,
For neither would want to stare.

She'd lay her hand right across her lap
Just so I could see the ring,
As if to say, 'I'm not yours today,
So don't hope for anything.'
But when she saw me looking her way
She'd raise her skirt to the thigh,
A look demure that would say, 'I'm pure,
I just like teasing your eye.'

And then one day it started to rain,
We sheltered under a tree,
We almost met, I'll never forget,
We stood as close as could be.

Her perfume wafted into my face
And that's when I should have said,
'It's such a shame, I don't know your name,
Your perfume's gone to my head.'

Her cheek was only a glance away
I think she knew my intent,
She glanced just once, and saw my dismay,
Then gave a look of contempt.
Since then she's been the wraith that I see
Reflected in streets and malls,
But could she have even wanted me?
The sense of my loss appals.

Fair Exchange

I probably failed to like the man
For he went with my ex-wife,
I hated the way she called him Stan,
As if he was hers for life.
They'd both been playing away from home
For a year, so said his ex,
I only heard from the grapevine bird
In a message of plain text.

'Your wife's been seeing my husband for
A year now,' said the note,
'If you'd like to know all the details
I can give them, creed and rote.'
I wandered round to the place she said
And she ushered me inside,
She said she wouldn't have bothered me
But suffered from wounded pride.

It seemed that they had been meeting
Every time I was away,
My job as a travelling salesman
Kept me on the road each day.
I'd be away for a week or more
But I thought that things were fine,
She didn't say that she'd let him play
With the things I thought were mine.

I couldn't believe he'd cheat on her,
When I looked at the wife of Stan,
She said that her name was Isabel
As she reached and squeezed my hand,

I thought that her face was beautiful
Though it bore the lines of stress,
She said she wanted revenge on them,
I couldn't have wanted less.

She said that she knew their routine, they
Would dine at the Globe Hotel,
Then go ahead and they'd book a room
At the neighbouring Motel,
I said I knew what we had to do
And we came up with a plan,
'I think we'll go and surprise them,
My wife and your husband Stan.'

We waited until they took their seats
At a table set for two,
Then wandered in and we said:
'We'll take this table, next to you.'
I'd never seen such spluttering, and
Each face turned beetroot red,
So then I kissed his wife, and turned
To Jane to say, 'You're dead!'

I'd only kissed her for effect
To see what Stan would do,
His face suffused with a jealous rage,
And Jane was jealous too,
It's since that day we've made a match
Both I and Isabel,
Which goes to show that a fair exchange
Can sometimes turn out well.

The Steersman

At night I walked in the winter months
By the banks of an old canal,
Where the barges lit their ghostly lamps
Like the wake of a funeral,
They would glide in those silent waters
With their silence like a shroud,
The horse at the end of the towrope
Passed me by, its head unbowed.

They sat so low in the water with
Their tons of pitch black coal,
The coal dust covered their livery
And of course, the paint was old,
A single steersman sat aloft
At the rear, and he looked ahead,
The black cut-out of a silhouette
Of a man that could be dead.

One night ahead of a hump-backed bridge
Where the towpath passed below,
The mist was a thick grey swirling mass
As the horse passed by me, slow,
I saw the glow of the ghostly lamp
And then as the barge appeared,
Just nosing out of the bank of fog
I thought that the bow looked weird.

For glistening under the ghostly lamp
And over the cabin door,
I saw a stream of something damp,
Was it mud, or blood, or gore?

I waited until the barge had passed
With the steersman, in my fright,
And I called out 'Bloody murder!
'You should look to your bow tonight.'

And the steersman muttered 'Carolyn',
In a voice both muted, low,
His voice came whispering back to me,
'She shouldn't have used me so.'
I saw his cardboard cut-out turn
In the glow of the ghostly lamp,
But then the barge slipped into the mist
Along with its bloody stamp.

I didn't know where it disappeared
On its voyage into the mist,
Along with its grisly cargo though
Its name was 'Amethyst',
But Carolyn lay aboard somewhere
In a pool of her blood as well,
As that barge would nose its way through mist
To enter the gates of hell.

The Google-up Ghost

'I've never believed in ghosts,' she said,
So I said, 'I'll prove there are.
I've seen them at night beside our bed,
I caught one sat in our car.
They wander along the street outside
I've seen them down at the beach,
You have to believe to see them, though,
They tend to be out of reach.'

'You'll have to produce one here for me
Before I'm going to believe,
It's easy to say that they exist
If you just want to deceive.'
She effectively threw the gauntlet down
So I just had to respond,
And work on a way to bring one here
From out the back of beyond.

But where do you go to find a ghost?
It's easier said than done,
I've seen so many of them, but most
Won't answer to anyone.
I thought I'd try to Google one up
When turning my PC on,
Then took a sip from my coffee cup
While typing in 'Ghost - just one.'

It threw up a series of single ghosts,
The one that walked in the rain,
And one that came with its head cut off,
A ghost in a railway train.

69

It even mentioned the woman in white
Who came halfway down the stair,
And stood by the bannister and groaned
With blood still thick in her hair.

I liked the thought of a railway train
With its own original ghost,
She didn't seem to be in much pain
So she appealed to me most.
I sent a message for meeting me where
She could come and meet the wife,
And bring the train, to give her a scare
That would last the rest of her life.

That night we lay in our poster bed
And I heard the shriek of wheels,
The wife rolled over as in it sped
The room was filled with her squeals.
The train pulled up by the bedroom door
And the ghost approached our bed,
She wore a nightdress, down to the floor
With bullet holes in her head.

'I've never believed in ghosts,' she'd said,
She'd have to believe them now,
The ghost approached with a look of dread,
And it caused a terrible row.
'Don't ever bring ghosts in here again
Or you'll be alone in the bed,'
As the train took off with a clicketty-clack
And the ghost just stood and bled.

I'm never allowed to Google up,
She said to stick to my verse,
They sit in the kitchen, while we sup
And even pass in the hearse,
She says that she never sees them now,
She doesn't want to believe,
I know it would only cause a row
If I said they tug at her sleeve.

Final Times

The rain came down in a torrent, while
The rest of the world had slept,
The mud it churned was abhorrent,
It was as if the planet wept.
They said we'd come to the final times
That the earth could take no more,
For people raged like a virus
Rotting the planet down to the core.

They said it's time that we left the place
That we found a pristine home,
It's sitting, somewhere out there in space
If we had the ship to roam.
But we're tied forever to walk the earth
And to share in its demise,
Or stop polluting, and rape, and looting
The place we live our lives.

For God is not going to save us now
Since he gave us all free will,
He won't be along to pick it up
The rubbish that we spill,

His temper's seen in the thunderheads
And the lightning in a storm,
The earthquake under our feet of clay
So we'll wish we'd not been born.

The final times have been coming since
The ancient days of Tyre,
And we, like them will be running from
Destruction, and from fire,
It's much too late to pontificate
On the things that should be done,
Before the planet's a wasted mass
On its journey around the sun.

Whenever the Mist...

The hoofbeats come through the mist at night
And the sound of clattering wheels,
While Ursula sits at the Inn in fright,
And we all know how that feels,
There's not been a coach for a hundred years
On these cobblestones, lining the lanes,
Not since the smugglers used a hearse
To carry their ill-gotten gains.

And though she may peer through the pebble glass
When the mist lies thick in the night,
She hopes that she'll see the phantom pass
But it's always out of sight,
A little beyond the light that beams
From the lamp that filters in,
To the darkened room in its haze of gloom
That they call the Smugglers Inn.

There's a story told from the days of old
When the customs lay in wait,
Their pistols drawn just before the dawn
When the hearse would meet its fate,
And Captain Sly with his one good eye
Was shot as he hit the ground,
While Ursula hears his cry of fear
As the customs gather round.

She only hears the scuffle of feet
And the neigh of a frightened horse,
That echoes out of the distant past
While the mist obscures its course,

But out, like a smear on the cobblestones,
And just where the Captain stood,
It takes a day just to fade away,
A pool of the Captain's blood.

It's only whenever a mist appears
That she hears the clattering wheels,
And thinks of death as she holds her breath
To know what the mist reveals,
For after the Captain has hit the ground
In front of the Smugglers Inn,
The door will open without a sound
For that's when the ghosts come in.

The Ice Log

I'd read of the yacht that was lost at sea,
Among the Antarctic ice,
I never thought it would matter to me
Though its ending wasn't so nice,
There were three on board, and two had died,
But one must have got away,
For I found the log of its final days
In a second-hand shop in the Bay.

It was badly damaged with damp and rot,
And some of the ink had run,
Some pages stuck so I couldn't read
The writing on every one.
But the hairs rose up on the back of my neck
To read what there was to see,
For a tale of human failings were what
Became so apparent to me.

They'd gone in search of the southern whales,
John Stanley, Evan and Eve,
Though why they went at that time of year
I find it hard to conceive,
For the winter's cruel in those Southern climes
And the sails ice up with the spray,
'It's hell when there's no-one to keep you warm,'
John Stanley wrote on the day.

For Evan and Eve kept each other warm,
While John made do with a quilt,
He wrote that Eve kept looking his way,
Could that be a sign of his guilt?

He waited till Evan had gone topside
Then made his advance to Eve,
But she just pushed him away, and then,
He wrote, 'I caught at her sleeve.'

'She fell, and crashed to the galley floor,
And split her head on the sink,
The wound on her scalp was red and raw,
I needed a moment to think.
I lifted her into an easy chair
And wiped the blood from her brow,
Then Evan came tumbling down the stair,
'What have you done to her now?'

The following entry was smeared with blood,
I couldn't read what it said,
I only know when he wrote again
That Evan must have been dead.
'I lifted him over the starboard rail
And slipped him into the sea,
His body had left a bloodied trail
But that had left Eve and me.'

'She came around on the second day,
But only could sit and stare,
So I lifted her into the lower bunk,
I needed her warmth in there.
A look of horror had crossed her face
When I crawled under the quilt,
And held her tight on that second night,
I can't explain how it felt.'

The next few pages were in a lump
I couldn't tear them apart,
But then a page was written in rage,
'I'd given the girl my heart.
But though she still couldn't speak to me
She lay on the bunk and spat,
I told her that Evan had gone, so she
Had better get over that.'

The ink had run on the following page
In water that looked like tears,
So he must have felt her rejection while
She lay, gave way to her fears.
The entry he wrote on the seventh day,
'I held her close, and she sighed,
I thought my love had begun to move her,
When I awoke, she'd died.'

'I held her close on the seventh night
But she had become so cold,
I tried to give her my body heat
As the yacht in the ocean rolled,
I couldn't slip her over the side
To do what I'd done before,
She needed a christian burial so
I'd take her back to the shore.'

The next few pages were merely rant
Bemoaning the love he'd lost,
But never a mention of Evan there,
Who'd paid the ultimate cost.

The sun came out on the fifteenth day
And the cabin became so warm,
Where Eve had lain in her rotting flesh
'The worms came out in a swarm.'

'I couldn't believe the smell down there,
Her body was falling apart,
I should have buried her when I could,
I just didn't have the heart.'
The yacht was locked in Antarctic ice
When the ice breaker came through,
And took both John and the Ice Log off,
So now I can read it to you.

But Eve lies still on the ice bound yacht
A skeleton now, but free,
Her soul in search of Evan, her love,
They'll meet down deep in the sea.
While John still roams abroad on the earth
And carries his personal hell,
To mourn the love that he found and lost
Among the Antarctic swell.

The Recalcitrant Hand

They put me in charge of the churchyard,
And said, 'mow between the graves,'
The weeds out there were atrocious
Grew in lumps, and clumps and waves,
They tangled up in the mower blades
And they shut the motor down,
So I had to use the garden shears
As I knelt upon the ground.

They covered some of the headstones, so
I had to rake them clear,
Spent half of my time sat reading them,
The date, the time of year,
The ground had given away on some,
Had fallen into a hole,
Wherever the coffin lids had caved
On some benighted soul.

The nights were coming on early so
I laboured into the dark,
Just by the light of a spirit lamp
That I'd borrowed from the park,
At length I came on a sunken grave
And I pulled the weeds aside,
To see the shape of a bony hand,
With the shock, I almost died.

The hand came up through the stoney earth
And it pointed to the sky,
With no flesh left on the fingers, yet
It seemed to question 'Why?'

It still belonged to the corpse below
But had tried to get away,
Out of the dark of doom and gloom
And into the light of day.

The name on the grave was 'Clarabelle'
And, 'She of the evil eye,
She hexed the cattle in Fingal's Dell
And the swine, while passing by,
They hung her high on a willow tree
When she pointed at Belle Raye,
Who choked, then withered and sighed, was dead,
And all in a single day.'

The hand had twitched, I couldn't resist
As I sat and watched it there,
I reached on out and I seized the wrist
And I felt some strange despair,
The hand was warm, and was then full-fleshed
As a shape rose from the ground,
That held me tight in the darkening light
With the hand that I had found.

I heard the rattle of death as she
Had tried to clear each lung,
Full of the body's liquid waste
That had formed when she was hung.
I heard a croak, and the words she spoke
As she glared into my face,
'I might be saved from my early grave,
But you'll have to take my place.'

Whatever power it was she had
It dissolved and turned to sand,
The moment I pulled away from her
And I let go of her hand.
She didn't speak, but let out a shriek
As she slid back in the grave,
So I'll never know if she heard below:
'You're much too bad to save!'

Jealousy

There was someone I detested at
The edges of my dream,
He was sneaky, underhanded and
I thought him quite unclean,
For he knew my life with Candace
Had then almost run its course,
He was waiting in the wings; I said,
'Don't take my wife by force.'

And he smiled, but somewhat grimly
In the way he had back then,
As if he would do whatever
To ensnare my wife again,
But I said, 'Don't even think it,
Though you had your chance before,
If you even make a move on her
It's like declaring war.'

He could tell then that I meant it
Just by looking in my eyes,
They were red, and so distended
That he backed off, he was wise,
But it didn't help my marriage
For her love had run its course,
And she told me in our carriage that
She wanted a divorce.

I had tried my best to please her
But my efforts went unsung,
I'd played hard to get, to tease her
Years before, when we were young,

And I'd won her then, from Anson
Who'd refused to go away,
And had hung around forever
Right up to the present day.

I had said it was unhealthy to have
Ex's hanging round,
But Candace said, 'He's just a friend,
Don't make him feel put down.'
She didn't think how I would feel
To always have him there,
At times when we should be alone,
He'd sit awhile, and stare.

So she left me on a Monday and
She barely said goodbye,
I wandered round the empty house
But found I couldn't cry,
For anger welled up in me when
I saw them walking past,
Arm in arm and laughing and
Together now, at last.

Emotions so intense rise up
To twist a jilted brain,
I swear I wasn't in control,
I must have been insane,
I traced them to his caravan
And waited till she left,
Then went to get some petrol
I was feeling so bereft.

I waited til the early hours
When he would be alone,
Then poured it underneath the door
Of this, his mobile home,
I thought, 'I'll fix his little scheme,'
And stood, and watched it pour,
Then lit it with a single spark,
It went up with a roar.

I had to stand and watch it then
The fruits of my despair,
I heard a scream, as in a dream
The door flung open there,
And Candace stood, encased in flame,
She shrivelled as she stood,
All black and burned, revenge had turned
Destroyed my neighborhood.

They didn't find too much of him
And she died on the grass,
They found me weeping in the gloom
When once the fire had passed,
And so I stare out blindly now
Through bars of hardened steel,
They wouldn't need to lock me in,
I've ceased to see or feel.

Blood and Gore

I wanted to write an amazing piece
That was like a sock on the jaw,
A classical piece like the Golden Fleece
In the Gothic form of yore,
But every time I am caught in rhyme
In the telling of every story,
And then it would have to be dark and bleak
With an ending that was gory.

The heroine would be bludgeoned down
By the boyfriend, who was jealous,
He'd always proclaimed that his love for her
Was pure, and clean, and zealous.
But came the day that she looked the way
Of a ripe and young Adonis,
The boyfriend knew, and his anger grew,
He was violent, to be honest.

The rhyme and rhythm would lead me on
To describe the blood in puddles,
Seeping out of her auburn hair
While his mind was full of muddles.
He saw the blood on the iron bar
That he held, he must have hit her,
But couldn't remember the fatal strike
And the thought just made him bitter.

Where could you go with a tale like that
Except to the judge and jury?
He put it down to the wine imbibed
And brought on the judge's fury.

He watched him put on the hanging cap
And he knew just what he'd got,
So pulled the gun from its hiding place
And that's how the judge was shot.

I'd like to say he was on the run
But a tale like that's suspicious,
How would he vault the wooden dock
In a place that's so judicious?
The sergeant actually gunned him down
To lie on the courtroom floor,
A pool would spread as he lay there dead,
Stretched out in his blood and gore.

And that's where we'll have to leave it now
For lack of a decent ending,
It wasn't such an amazing piece
And I know it's needed mending.
But rhyme and metre has bogged me down
To give a twist to my story,
I'll try to do better next time around
With a tale that's not so hoary.

The Tunnel to Hell

There'd been stories about a tunnel
In the old, Victorian house,
We didn't know where it led to,
But were keen on finding out,
It opened into a passageway
From a library wall of books,
Was dark, and damp and foreboding
If you merely went by looks.

To us it had spelt adventure,
To Jeremy Coates and me,
'As long as we take a flashlight,'
I'd said to Jeremy,
We waited till after midnight
When the others were asleep,
We didn't want to involve them all
Till we had taken a peep.

'What do you think we'll find there?'
He said as we opened the door,
Pushing aside a shelf of books
To stand on a flagstoned floor,
The passage led down a flight of steps
All green, and covered in moss,
We'd ventured in to this place of sin
On the date of Pentecost.

We should have known what we'd find there
If we'd taken note of the books,
The ones on the sliding bookshelf
And hidden in crannies and nooks,

There was more than a single Grimoire,
And the Oera Linda book,
That was known as Himmler's Bible,
If we'd only taken a look.

There were copies of the Picatrix,
And the Munich Manual,
The first bore spells in Arabic,
The next strange animals,
There were books on demonology
Black magic spells as well,
And even a long chronology
Of the many circles of hell.

We ventured into that passageway
Not knowing any of this,
No doubt, if only we'd read them all
We wouldn't be risking this,
But on we marched in the dead of night
To follow the flashlight beam,
Where the walls oozed iridescent streams
And the smell was quite obscene.

We walked a mile through the tunnel
Where it ended in a crypt,
With panels through to the street level
That would keep it dimly lit,
But this was night and the only light
Beamed in through the pillar flutes,
From the gas lamps out on the cobbled street
By the church known as St. Lukes.

And all around there were catafalques
Where the coffins lay in state,
Down in this modern catacomb
Where the devil lay in wait,
For a goat's head sat on the further wall
By an altar, scarred and scored,
With the shapes of naked women who
Were seen as the devil's whores.

A cross was stood on the altar but
It was mounted upside down,
Ready to celebrate black mass
In this hidden underground,
Then just as we stood and took this in
A coffin had raised its lid,
And Jeremy screamed a terrible scream
While I ran round and hid.

A shape rose up in a long black cloak
That had eyes of instant fire,
Teeth that could rip a corpse to shreds
In a moment of desire,
For evil never had looked so dark
As the horns on that spectre's head,
While Jeremy screamed just one last scream
And fell by the coffin, dead.

I don't remember how I survived
My flight up that passageway,
I'd thrown all caution to the winds
When I heard the spectre say:

'Who dares to sully my sanctum, and
Disturb my sated sleep,
I've roamed abroad for a thousand years
That the seeds I've sown will keep.'

I reached the end of that passageway
And I slid the shelves across,
All of those books were glowing now
With the innocence I'd lost,
And then I heard but a mile away
Was the tolling of a bell,
Up in the belfry of St. Lukes
That covered the path to hell.

The Steamer

We picked up a coal-fired steamer
From a graveyard of ancient ships,
It had lain, beached up in the Philippines,
Sat on the rusted slips,
The ship was covered in surface rust
But it hadn't gone right through,
So with elbow grease and some paint at least
My friend said, 'It will do.'

We registered it in Colombia,
And we flew the Colombian flag,
We couldn't afford to insure it,
And Derek said, 'That's a drag.
But we only need a single trip
And a cargo in the hold,
Like tractor tyres and some copper wires,
We'll be rich when they are sold.'

He brought his girlfriend, Mary Anne,
Which I thought was a mistake,
He said that she'd come in handy when
We had to cook and bake.
'I hope that she's not bad luck for us,'
I muttered, when she came,
'You mean those superstitious tales
That a woman is to blame?'

The bosun hired was a Robert Legg
Who had been at sea for years,
We didn't know, as the trip would show,
He'd bring my friend to tears.

He helped to paint the rusted hull
In just one colour, black,
But leered when Mary Anne appeared
And behind Derek's back.

We hired a couple of Lascars
To shovel in the coal,
Then ventured out for a cargo,
And ended up in Seoul,
We picked up a dodgy cargo,
Enough to make a run,
Over to western Africa
With computers, and with guns.

We named the ship the 'Avant Garde'
And we braved the ocean swell,
It rolled and creaked, and even leaked
Like the cargo ship from hell,
But Derek's mood was grim and dour
As we fought to hold the wheel,
'Let's hope that it doesn't fall apart,
There's a buckle in the keel.'

We spent our time up on the bridge
With Mary Anne below,
It doesn't take a genius
To know how that would go.
For Legg spent too much time down there
Ensconced with Mary Anne,
When Derek questioned her, she said,
'The bosun's quite the man.'

He sent Legg down to the engine room
And he said to keep his place,
He wasn't there for a holiday
Or to chat up a friendly face.
But Legg was sour, and Derek dour
When he caught them down below,
And said Legg's hand was in contraband
Where he knew it shouldn't go.

The Avant Garde had then burst a seam
Just above the waterline,
The water had started slopping in
We knew we were short on time,
By then Legg quarrelled with Derek, said
His girl was a free for all,
Was there to satisfy base desires,
Derek pinned him against the wall.

He hit the bosun across the head
With a long steel marlin spike,
Who fell at once and was good and dead,
I was told to take a hike.
I think he carted the body down
To the lascars down below,
Who bundled him into the furnace there,
No corpse, so who's to know?

He told me later he'd fixed the leak
But he didn't tell me how,
The ship then shuddered against a rock
That bent and burst the prow,

Before it sank I went down below
To witness a nightmare scene,
The body of Mary Anne was jammed
In tight, where it sealed the seam.

Home from the Lake

I just got home in the past half hour
From a great weekend at the lake,
I can't remember how I got home,
I think I'm about to flake.
The driveway's empty, I lost the car,
The house, as quiet as a tomb,
And where the wife and the kiddies are?
Must be in another room.

The air round here had been highly charged
For weeks, till we got away,
So I suggested a trip from home
If only just for a day.
I thought we could sort our problems out
Just for our marriage's sake,
I thought that we might find love again
Together, up at the lake.

The kids took buckets and floaties too,
They said that it would be fun,
And Jen took some of her own home brew,
She's legless, after just one.
We packed them all in the four wheel drive
And headed up for the shack,
It's on a reach that they call the beach,
It took an hour to unpack.

But Jen got drunk, as she always does
And spoiled the night of the first,
Her mood was black, while on the attack,
I said our marriage was cursed.

I saw no love in her eyes that night,
And even her smile was forced,
So stone cold sober the second day
She said, 'I want a divorce.'

I thought that she might get over it,
I said, 'We're here to have fun.
Let's call a truce for the kids at least,
Be happy, for everyone.'
She said she would, but she wouldn't talk,
Just glowered, down at the beach,
While I and the kids would take a walk,
Have fun in the sun, at least.

Now in the drive, I can see a car,
A man has come to the door,
He says, 'We pulled out your four wheel drive,
What did you do it for?'
I look bemused as he says to me,
'Your children, for heaven's sake!'
My heart stops for an infinity,
'You drowned them all in the lake.'

The Seabed Wreck

I like to dive on a sunken wreck
If the sea is not too rough,
The seabed's littered with carcasses
I never can get enough,
They range from the Roman caravel,
With the huge, high mounted prow,
To the dinosaurs of steel, from wars,
Still roaming the oceans now.

Some of them lie not far offshore
So the water's not too deep,
I can trail an oxy line down there
Up to a hundred feet,
But a scuba tank I would have to thank
For the freedom to explore,
Deep in the bowels of a sunken ship
In the search for gold moidores.

I dived one blustery Autumn day
In a well known coastal rip,
The sea rose up and carried me off
Away from my chosen ship,
But through the gloom of that Autumn storm
There loomed an exciting shape,
The remains of a Spanish Galleon,
Blown way off course by the Cape.

All I could see was the galleon stern
With the Bon-Adventure mast,
Broken off and above the mud
It had settled in, at last,

97

I wriggled in through a window frame
And I found the Captain's den,
Complete with the Captain's skull and bones
Back from I don't know when.

The figure sat at a writing desk
Sprawled in an ancient chair,
The wood of each was well preserved
And so was the Captain's hair,
A flintlock pistol lay on the desk
Next to the dead man's hand,
A bullet hole in the bleached white skull
As the ship sank into the sand.

I knew that gold lay under the mud,
I'd have to come back and search,
But just as the storm was blowing up
The galleon gave a lurch,
It freed itself from its clinging grave
And started to float away,
And I swam out as it disappeared,
Lost to this very day.

For somewhere under the heaving sea
It sails, but under the swell,
Back where its sailors sailed before
When they were consigned to hell.
It roams abroad with its hoard of gold
And may well settle again,
Along with its phantom Captain, but
Will never be seen by men.

The Mantle Clock

I found I was left a mantle clock
The type that you wind by key,
It had stood upon my father's shelf,
Now it came down to me.
Inside the clock I had found a note
Scrawled in my father's hand,
'You never must overwind the clock
For time is a shifting sand.'

That's all that it said, that tiny note
And I'd wondered what he meant,
Surely he could have talked to me
And made it more evident.
But my father had been secretive
And never would say too much,
Just that his life had raced away
And left him behind, and such.

The end of his life had come too soon,
It certainly was a shock,
I found him sat alone in his chair
And pointing up at the clock,
It wasn't until the afternoon
I noticed the clock had stopped,
Just as his heart had ceased to beat,
There wasn't a tick, or tock.

I took it home and I placed it up
In pride of place on the shelf,
Over the wooden mantlepiece
And wound the thing up myself.

I just didn't know how many times
I was meant to turn the key,
So probably over wound it then,
Not knowing what was to be.

Over the following week I found
The clock had been gaining time,
And thought, that's probably what he meant,
Never to over wind,
I tried to adjust it back a bit
To change the rate of the pawl,
But found the cog was racing away
And speeding up overall.

No matter what I did to that clock
Its speed just wouldn't be tamed,
I'd slow it down and it speeded up,
I felt I was being gamed,
But then I woke on a Wednesday and
I thought there was something strange,
The man on the news said 'Thursday',
Like the days had been rearranged.

The weeks and the months went flying by,
I still kept winding that clock,
Remembering how my father died,
I wouldn't have dared to stop.
But then one day I forgot to wind
And it slowed, and took me aback,
I held the key, was about to wind
When I had my heart attack.

Luckily Joyce was in the room
Thank god for my lovely wife,
She seized the key and she wound it up
And probably saved my life.
I never forget to wind it now
That clock's in sync with my heart,
But now my life is racing away
With the clock still playing its part.

Madame La Guillotine

I asked the woman where she came from,
She didn't utter a word,
But stood outside on the landing where
She wouldn't be seen, or heard.
She glided into the bedroom then
And dropped her gown on the floor,
Then climbed up onto the four poster
A thing I couldn't ignore.

The name embroidered upon the gown
Was one, a Lucie La Corte,
It lay there crumpled upon the ground,
A thing of beauty, I thought,
But far more beautiful, there she lay
Within the reach of my hand,
With silken skin that had reeked of sin
Inviting love on demand.

I caught the scent of wisteria
The fragrance rose from her breast,
I felt close to hysteria,
Like I was put to the test,
I lay and stared at her shapely form
And thought, how could I resist,
But then I noticed the branding mark
An ugly Fleur de lis.

It sat high on her shoulder there
To tell what she had done,
Some grim crime from another time
And an execution…

I heard her sigh as she raised one thigh
Then I saw her eyes had teared,
Her teardrops fell, and she broke the spell
For then she had disappeared.

If ever you're visiting Paris
And those evil streets, and mean,
Beware, the hotel you stay is not
Called 'Madame La Guillotine',
Or you may lie in a poster bed
As I did, god help the thought,
And watch as the visitor sidles in
The one, a Lucie La Corte.

Thunder & Lightning

The night was a night of thunder,
Of flashes of lightning too,
Her eyes had stared out in wonder
At what it was going to do.
She stood by the attic window
To stare outside in a trance,
While out in the breeze, the wind in the trees
Would flutter, and leap, and dance.

The bolts had zig-zagged like dragons
That fought in the eastern sky,
They carried their battle wagons
Of fireworks, sparked on high.
But now and then with a force like zen
They'd crash to earth on the ground,
And blight the night with a fierce light
And a most tumultuous sound.

It rattled the attic windows,
The shutters blew out like a sail,
The rain pit-pattered each window pane
And suddenly turned to hail.
The wind was humming and crooning
As it flitted up in the eaves,
The parting clouds let the moon in,
Tracing a path through the trees.

And she remembered the tales she'd heard
Of the thunder god named Thor,
Who beat with his mighty hammer
Downstairs on the outside door.

The wind was warbling, 'Let me in,'
In a tone that meant to entice,
But Barbara shivered alone in her skin,
She wouldn't be caught out twice.

For once she'd opened the outside door
In a storm when she was young,
And stood on the outside paving stones
When the lightning danced on her tongue.
And dragons crackled across her brain
While lightning flashed from her eyes,
'Just come outside, there will be no pain,'
The wind was telling her lies.

She stood so close to the window pane
She wasn't prepared for the flash,
A blinding light almost took her sight,
Her image was burnt on the glass.
And now if you stand in the garden there
Look up to the attic room,
And Barbara still stares down at you
Though she's been long in her tomb.

She'd turned away from the window pane
And staggered down by the stair,
She was almost blind but she had to find
Just who was calling her there.
The outside door swung open and wide
She stepped on the paving stones,
And Thor delivered a hammer blow
That shattered Barbara's bones.

On Waking...

You wake on a bitter morning,
To find that your love is lost,
You turn your head to an empty bed
On the eve of Pentecost.
You reach on out to feel the warmth
That was there in the days of old,
But now, in that empty space you find
That the sheets and the bed are cold.

And then you remember the night before
And that terrible tête à tête,
When you both dug deep for the love you lost
But all you could feel was hate.
You'd always sworn you would make it up
Before you went off to bed,
That chance was lost, now you count the cost
As demons roam in your head.

You think that your partner must recall
All the love that you've made till now,
On searching your head, that love is dead,
So how to remember... How?
The eyes that used to adore you, now
Have narrowed down to slits,
The mouth turned down at the corners that
Would pout, as you kissed those lips.

Love is a short term happiness
That doesn't transpire for long,
For love will frown as it's beaten down
And comes to the end of the song.

You wait in vain by the open door
In hopes that it reappears,
But time moves on, and you know they've gone,
The end of the tale is tears.

The Congenital Liar

Have ever you noticed that liars
Cross their fingers when they lie?
They seem to think it absolves them from
A judgement, up on high,
For fingers crossed means they didn't mean
The thing they're telling you,
But if you're silly, and fall for it
They make you think it's true.

I knew a terrible liar once
His name was John Coltrane,
He always cried on my shoulder then
As if he was in pain,
He said that life was short-changing him,
That there was nothing fair,
It only took just a minor thing
To drive him to despair.

We both worked then at an auto plant
And used a giant press,
Knocking out doors and bonnets there,
And working under stress,
For time and motion had set a rate
That we could not fulfil,
And truth to tell it had seemed like hell
And was making Coltrane ill.

No matter how fast we put them through
The steel kept banking up,
Thanks to the other press's crew
Who'd stop, and have a cup,
While we were struggling then to clear
The backlog, piled up high,
And John was constantly in my ear,
'I think I want to die.'

I said that he didn't mean it,
It was just a lousy job,
But he just kept on repeating it
And even began to sob,
To tell the truth, it got on my nerves,
It really began to grate,
I lost my cool, and I said the fool
Was really tempting fate.

He seemed to go a bit crazy then,
Lay backwards on the dye,
I tried to pull him away, but he
Lay staring at the sky,
The press came down with a mighty thump
And it flattened out his head,
Two hundred and fifty tons per inch
Said John Coltrane was dead.

We all of us stood around in shock
When the press released him there,
All that was left was a headless corpse
With blood and brains to spare,

His corpse let out a terrible sigh
At the judgement he had lost,
For though he said he would want to die,
He lay with his fingers crossed.

The Restless Wife

The storm had unleashed its fury,
In gales, on the night before,
Had scribbled its bitter story
All over a battered shore,
For there lay the yacht 'Imagine',
Cast up on the outer reef,
Its sails and its stays were sagging,
And shredded beyond belief.

I scrambled over the rocks out there
When the tide left it high and dry,
In hopes that I'd find my friend, Jo Bère,
Unhurt, though I don't know why.
Jo Bère was such a mountainous man
And so much larger than life,
He'd sailed through many a perfect storm
On board, with his restless wife.

So when I clambered aboard that day
I heard her calling my name,
And something about her pitiful cry
Said nothing would be the same.
I found her down on the cabin floor
All bruised, and somewhat distressed,
The storm had shattered the cabin door
And left the cabin a wreck.

I said to Dawn, 'you outlived the storm,
But where is my friend, Jo Bère?'
She said, 'He fell overboard last night,
I looked for him everywhere.'
Though she was bruised, there wasn't a cut,
Just thrown around in the flood,
So what was the smear on the locker there,
The ominous sign of blood?

'He must have fallen and hit his head,
I can't remember, I swear,
The yacht was tossed and my husband lost,
He must be floating out there.'
I knew that she was a restless wife
She'd often give me the eye,
I knew their marriage had been in strife,
Could never figure out why.

But now she reached and she held my hand
And gave it a gentle squeeze,
'My husband's gone, but my life goes on,
I'll always be here to please.
You must know, I've always cared for you,'
I said, 'Don't ever go there,
Because, to me, you will always be
The wife of my friend, Jo Bère.'

Her face grew dark, and I saw the spark
Of an anger, much like a storm,
She didn't take to rejection well,
And I should have been forewarned.

I turned to leave so that I could grieve
The loss of my friend, Jo Bère,
Then saw on the floor the bloodstained axe,
With clumps of my old friend's hair.

She leapt for it, but I got there first,
And I stamped it, down on the floor,
Then Dawn was wild, like a crazy child,
She came at me, tooth and claw.
'I never thought you would murder him,'
I cried, while beating her off,
She screamed, 'You're not going to put me in,'
And then she started to laugh.

A high pitched laugh that was like a scream
As I clambered over the side,
Just as the sea was flooding in,
Right at the turn of the tide.
She must have known that she'd have to pay
When I told them, creed and rote,
For I heard them say, the following day,
'That woman has cut her throat.'

The Way it Is...

'What are we going to do with you?'
My parents would say to me,
'We want you to work in a banking house,
But you write poetry.
You may look back on a wasted life
If that was all you did,
You need to steady, and take a wife
So you'll need to make a quid.'

While I, in all of my innocence
Would look at them, askance,
'If life were just about money, then
I think I'd rather dance.
I don't believe that it's all about
The grind, amassing wealth,
I cast my fate to the winds, let that
Take care of it, itself.'

I needed to be creative so
I scribbled, more and more,
Composing the perfect poems that
Did not exist before,
They didn't earn me a single quid
But that was not the plan,
A part of me will be left behind
Once I am done with man.

And so I tell the Millennials
Don't waste your time with sweat,
But add something to your culture that
Has not been written yet,
Whether your art is writing, music,
Painting, poetry,
The question, 'What will *you* do with you?'
In time, will set you free.

The Whispering Tree

I knew that I shouldn't be driving,
I'd had one more for the road,
So Jean and me were half cut, you see,
Were carrying quite a load.
We'd tried the Tequila slammers,
I'd even swallowed the worm,
I wish to hell I had lost the key
Then we'd both be home, and warm.

The road was most uninviting,
Was glistening in the dark,
We climbed on into the Beamer,
And headed out of the park.
The rain was a constant drizzle
As the Moon peeked over the trees,
I know that I should have listened
When Jean would entreat me, 'Please!'

She always said that I drove too fast
And she was probably right,
I slammed my foot down flat to the boards
And sped away through the night.
The headlights cut a swathe through the trees
And lit the road in an arc,
I thought that we were invincible,
Speeding home in the dark.

It must have been a tyre that blew,
The Beamer suddenly veered,
The car careened off the road, it seemed,
No matter how I had steered.

It seemed to leap at a grove of trees
And hit the oak at a lean,
I was safe with my seatbelt on,
But Jean had flown through the screen.

She'd been sat quietly, holding my hand,
Her warmth was all that I felt,
She'd whispered softly her words of love,
Forgotten to put on her belt.
Now she lay spread on the bonnet there
Her head crushed into the tree,
I hoped and prayed, but I didn't dare
Step out of the wreck, to see.

And then I heard her whispering words
Float back through the shattered screen,
'If only you had listened to me…'
I said, 'I know what you mean.'
'You know our love was a special love,'
She seemed to whisper afar,
'Just know my love will always be there,
I'll beam it down from a star.'

My life is cold, and empty as well,
Since ever my love was lost,
I carry around my private hell
In a heart that is tempest tossed.
For now I know that I have no choice
When it all comes back to me,
If ever I need to hear her voice
I go to the whispering tree.

Spooking a Spook

They didn't tell when we bought the place
Of the ghost in the attic room,
They knew that they'd have to drop the price
If the spook jumped out in the gloom.
So we'd signed the papers and paid the fees,
There wasn't really an out,
We'd had a couple of days of peace
Then it came jumping about.

It started with a terrible crash
That roused us out of our bed,
I said, 'that sounded like breaking glass
And it came from overhead.'
But overhead was the attic room
And that was an empty space,
So I went up with a whisking broom,
Found glass, all over the place.

And worse than that, it was mirror shards
It was seven years bad luck,
So just like an irritated Bard
I yelled out, 'WTF?'
I got to work with the whisking broom
And was cursing, fit to toss,
When the spook, in the corner of the room
Appeared with a blazing cross.

I noticed he held it upside down
Raised up, to cover his face,
I must admit that I threw a fit,
I acted with little grace,

'What the hell are you doing here,
You've given us quite a fright,
Don't you know, we were trying to sleep,
It's an hour past midnight.'

It waved the blazing cross in the air
And gave out a dreadful groan,
Then flames from the floor devoured him
And left me standing alone.
I went back down to the bedroom to
The woman I loved the most,
Who said, 'Well, what did you find up there?'
'We've got us a Holy Ghost!'

From that night on, it was every night
It was boom and crash and groan,
While Jenny in fright, would curl up tight,
'Won't he ever leave us alone?'
I said, "It's only at night he comes,
He must sleep during the day,
I have an idea, don't worry dear,
He won't have it all his way.'

I rigged up a speaker system there
And fed it all through an amp,
Then during the day, I'd blast away
And light the room with a lamp,
A blinding lamp of a thousand watts
To strobe, at a hundred clicks,
And blasted him with Metallica,
I knew it would make him sick.

The spook came out on the seventh day
Stood trembling on the stair,
The flames on his cross had all gone out,
He stood there, tearing his hair.
He dashed on out through the open door
I thought he was going to puke,
And that was the last of the Ghost we saw,
So that's how you spook a Spook!

Time Waits for No Man

'The time's become fleeting and flying,
And rushing me off to the grave,'
Or so would say Roderick Styling,
'It's sweeping me on like a wave.'
I found his remarks so depressing
I'd walk on the side of the street
Where I knew he wouldn't be walking,
On hearing the sound of his feet.

He'd corner me back in the office,
Unburden his pure misery,
Or catch me in field or in coppice,
To tell me his bleak history.
For often I'd find he was waiting
Wherever he shouldn't have been,
I found that I couldn't avoid him,
His whispers and chatter obscene.

'We've only one life, so enjoy it,'
I'd counter, when he would begin,
But then he would start to destroy it,
By saying that life became grim.

'The older you get, so the faster,
It races along like a train,
Is headed for certain disaster,
The end of the journey is pain.'

Then he seemed to age by the minute,
His skin became wrinkled and worn,
Despair, he would seem to dive in it,
And had since the day he was born.
'You'll not do yourself any favours,'
I'd say, 'when it hangs on each breath,
For life will not gift what it savours,
If you're so determined on death.'

But one day I looked in the mirror,
And saw what I never had seen,
The markings of age, like a river,
Were flowing, where once youth had been.
I tried to ignore it by sighing
That ageing was lending me grace,
But I could see Roderick Styling
Was staring right back in my face.

And that's when I knew life was fleeting
I had to seize what there was left,
I sent him a note for a meeting
While I was still feeling bereft.
He lies in a grave in a coppice
A jagged hole under his jaw,
While I work alone, in the office,
He'd got what he'd been looking for.

Do or Dare

I watched her dance with her bright red crop
At a party of Do or Dare,
Strutting her stuff on a table top
I knew I could have her there.
For she mouthed at me, 'You're the only one,'
As she stripped right down to the buff,
I mouthed, 'You're on,' but she still danced on
I'd never have seen enough.

While all the others would reach and grope
I stood well back and I stared,
She tipped champagne all over their heads
All over the ones that dared,
She fell down into my open arms
Once she had finished her dance,
While Emma Lou took her place up there,
But I'd found a new romance.

I'd gone to the party for Emma Lou
Who'd wanted to meet me there,
She'd said, 'I feel like taking a chance,
The party's a Do or Dare.'
We'd only dated a month or two
But that hadn't got too far,
We'd gone for drinks at the Seven Links
And necked in the back of the car.

But Carla Deane was a ginger dream
For flames had danced in her hair,
The prettiest body I'd ever seen,
I knew she wanted to share,

For in my arms I could feel her charms
And she raised her lips for a kiss,
Her silken skin promised treats within
And who was I to resist?

She dressed again, it was almost ten
When she took me home to her flat,
And poured a couple of highballs, then
She suddenly said, 'That's that!'
It seems her wager with Emma Lou
Said she could steal me away,
If she could, anyone else could too,
She didn't intend to play.

I felt like the dog with a juicy bone
Stood staring into a stream,
And seeing my own reflection there
I'd dropped the bone for a dream.
For Emma Lou never came to call
The bone I'd managed to drop
For one swept over a waterfall
Who'd danced on a table top.

Twin Paths

The day had been rather stormy when
I walked in the garden gate,
With lighting flashing around me,
It was dark, and getting late.
I tried the key in the old front door
But found that it didn't fit,
And had to pound on the knocker so
That Kate would answer it.

It took a minute or so before
I heard her steps on the floor,
She probably wondered who it was
Before she opened the door,
She stared at me with the strangest look
On her face that I'd ever seen,
But stood there blocking the door, I said,
'Aren't you going to let me in?'

She stood aside in a moment then
And I walked in through the door,
She said, 'And what's the occasion then?
You've not called here before.'
I thought she must have been joking then
And gave her a sickly smile,
She said, 'you'd better believe it, you
Have not been here for a while.'

I tried to give her a kiss, but she
Pulled back, and turned away,
'The time for that was an age ago,
That was another day.'

I asked her what she had meant, for she
Had been my wife for years,
'Not since you married my sister, and
You turned my world to tears.'

I said that I didn't follow her,
And must have looked confused,
She said that I'd turned my back on her
And left her feeling used,
'You broke off from our engagement, when
The date had just been set,
And went and married my sister then,
You're married to Jeanette.'

I thought I was going crazy, though
Perhaps, I thought, it's Kate,
Having a mid-life crisis, but she
Looked at me with hate.
She said to go to her sister's place
Just further down the street,
So thinking that I would humour her
I went, through hail and sleet.

I tried my key in Jeanette's front door
And that gave me a shock,
The key had fitted it perfectly
As then the door unlocked,
I wandered into the kitchen where
Jeanette was making tea
For a man at the kitchen table,
But I swear that the man was me!

The Wind in the Wires

She went with a friend for the evening,
But she wouldn't tell me where to,
Just turned as the two began leaving,
Said, 'Where I go's nothing to you.'
She liked to be so independent,
Go off, and leave me on the spot,
Then tried to make me feel repentant
For asking her why, where or what?

I sat up and waited till midnight,
Expecting that she would be home,
She must have known I would be uptight
Not knowing where she'd gone to roam.
I knew that her friend never liked me,
Would glory in turning the screw,
Encourage Darlene to defy me,
She'd tell her, 'So what can he do?'

She hadn't returned the next morning,
Nor even when it became noon,
The sun towards eve began falling,
So surely she must return soon.
I passed the time on the computer,
Watched Facebook alive on the screen,
When Darlene popped up using FaceTime
Then suddenly started to scream.

'You'll have to come in here and get me,
I seem to be inside my phone,
I tried leaving, it wouldn't let me,
And Marge went and left me alone.'

The face on the screen began fraying,
And she was hysterical now,
Her face in the picture was greying,
'I'll come for you, just tell me how.'

'Just follow me through all the windows,
The frames are all breeding like spores,
My mind's in a haze, I'm caught in a maze,
There's many more windows than doors.'
I looked for her picture in Instagram,
And searched for her trace in What's App,
Then Googled her name, she ran through a frame,
But all that I caught was her back.

The high tension wires running overhead
Were humming and whining all night,
I lay in my bed, convinced she was dead,
Then heard her voice moaning in fright.
The Darlene I knew never came back home,
She travels by churches and spires,
A crackle in time and a hum in the line
Tells me she is the Wind in the Wires.

Three Days in a Cave

We were on a tour of the Breton Caves
That had stalactites galore,
A one-time trip to that limestone drip
Forming stalagmites on the floor.
There were only eight, and the tour was late
Was the last one for the day,
It was getting dark in the tourist park
But the guide still led the way.

And that's when I first saw Monica
Who hung on her boyfriend's arm,
There was something about her, even then
Some quiet, ineffable charm.
I tried to speak, to engage her there
But she snubbed each tame advance,
And flashed the ring on her finger that
Proclaimed her one romance.

The party wandered about the caves,
Spread out on the limestone floor,
And even Monica wandered off
For what she was looking for.
So when the ceiling had tumbled in
Creating a great divide,
With she and I all alone in there,
The rest on the other side.

The only light was a single beam
That came through a crack above,
And Monica stood in fear, and screamed,
Called out to her new-found love.

But he was stuck on the other side
Of a thousand tons of stone,
I told her, he couldn't hear a thing,
She said, 'Just leave me alone.'

She treated me with a great disdain
As if it had been my fault,
That she'd been caught on the further side
At the drop of the limestone vault.
I said, 'We're lucky to be alive,
It's better than being dead,
Under a thousand tons of rock,
Get that in your pretty head!'

The beam then slowly faded away
And left us sat in the dark,
I heard her sigh, and begin to cry,
Our future was bleak and stark.
I thought that I'd try to comfort her
But she pushed my hand away,
'Don't let my fears give you sick ideas,
We'll be out of here in a day.'

That was a long and lonely night
And the worst, by far, of three,
'They may come looking for you,' I said,
'There's no-one looking for me.'
'Haven't you got a girl at home?'
She ventured, one little spark,
Said in an almost friendly tone
As we lay there in the dark.

We heard the skittering sound of rats
As I said, 'No, I'm alone.'
And then she suddenly came up close,
'I'm sorry,' was in her tone.
We shared a couple of chocolate bars,
I sensed her shivering form,
And threw my coat round her shoulders then
Just trying to keep her warm.

The beam appeared as the sun came up,
She finally met my eyes,
'I'm sorry if I was off before,
You seem to be kind, and wise.'
'I simply think that you're beautiful,'
I said, with a touch of awe,
'Your guy must think you're incredible.'
'I wish…,' and she softly swore.

The hours dragged by, and a day and night
Seemed more than a week to me,
'Maybe they think, on the other side
We're buried, so let us be.'
The pangs of hunger were bad by now
And nothing to slake our thirst,
'If only I'd known,' said Monica,
'I'd never have come, we're cursed.'

The cold got us on the second night,
She didn't resist me much,
My coat we draped over both of us,
I felt the warmth of her touch.

Her head was lying across my chest
My arms held her, in bliss,
And that's when she raised her face to me
And gave me a gentle kiss.

Three days we lay there in misery,
We felt that it was the end,
'If we're to die, then I wonder why
I'd not make love with a friend?'
The thought of death fairly takes the breath
There's things we wouldn't have done,
But she was as eager as me, you see,
In coming together as one.

They broke on through in the afternoon
Of the third day after the fall,
And there her guy with a glistening eye
As she climbed over the wall.
They took us both to the hospital
And I thought she had gone for good,
A brief respite in a lonely life,
But suddenly, there she stood.

I felt bemused and a mite confused
When I asked her, 'Where's your guy?'
She shrugged and said we were almost dead,
While he was as sweet as pie.
'He didn't share my imprisonment,
So what did you want to do?
It only took three days in a cave,
I've fallen in love with you.'

The Wander

She used to walk in the woods at night,
She said she needed the air,
But didn't want me to go with her,
She said that it's cold out there.
'Well, cold for me would be cold for you,'
I said, but she didn't mind,
'I need to go on my own,' she said,
Made out she was being kind.

Though what it was I would find, who knew?
It raised suspicions in me,
For what do you meet in a darkened wood
But only the occasional tree?
Perhaps she wasn't the only one
Who wandered into the sward,
Maybe another lonely one,
But no, she gave me her word.

Not that her word was worth too much
As I'd caught her out before,
Meeting a man delinquently,
But never again, she swore.
I had no reason to doubt her then
She said she would play it square,
'It's only an empty wood,' she said,
'There's nothing but trees out there.'

I followed her into the woods one night,
Kept quietly out of sight,
And watched as she entered a clearing,
Deep in the dead of night.

She walked straight up to an old ash tree
And knelt before it, and prayed,
While fronds from the tree encircled her,
Like some strange masquerade.

And then as I watched, a shape appeared
Embedded within the tree,
The form of a man, the god named Pan
As clear as it could be.
Patricia advanced, embraced him now
And the form sprang into life,
Doing the things you wouldn't do
Except with a much loved wife.

He looked like a goat that stood erect,
His horns swept back from his head,
Balancing on his cloven hoofs
While I hid myself in dread.
He raised a set of pipes to his lips
And played an enchanting tune,
That swept the glade as Patricia played
And cavorted in the gloom.

Then suddenly I was back at home,
Woke up in my easy chair,
I rubbed my eyes to the sound of sighs
And Patricia was standing there.
'I just had the strangest dream,' I said,
'Of you in a woodland glade.'
And she just smiled for a little while
As I sat in my chair, dismayed.

'I think I know why you wander now,
Though you never will with me,
There's something about a clearing there
And a most remarkable tree.'
She turned, and pierced me with a look
That said that she didn't care,
'It's true, I have a favourite nook
Where I go… I saw you there!'

Coconut Ice

She lived in a strange old gabled house
But she rarely came outside,
I'd glimpse her up on the balcony
But she'd see me, and she'd hide.
She seemed a nervous, tremulous thing
But I thought she looked so sweet,
Her hair in a long blonde ponytail,
And a dimple in either cheek.

She lived alone with her grandmother
Who was old, and sharp of tongue,
A sort of witch with a constant itch
She had scratched since she was young.
She wouldn't allow young callers, who
Attracted to Abigail,
Would try to court but were overwrought
By her, till their efforts failed.

The two who had breached her sanctuary
Who had forced their way inside,
Had only stayed but a single day
Then emerged, and had later died.
It seemed that a curse lay on that house
There was something in the air,
A sense of sin that had lain within
Caught up in the word, 'despair'.

The more that I glimpsed of Abigail,
The more that my heart would leap,
I'd stand and stare on the corner there
And I'd sometimes hear her weep.

I'd hear the drone of that dry old crone
As she snapped and snarled at her,
'A man is a fret that you'll soon regret,
There's a thousand more out there.'

I finally braved the woman's wrath
And beat on their old front door,
I knew she wouldn't invite me in
But hoped that her mood would thaw.
'I'm coming to call on Abigail,'
I cried, and I pushed on past,
And racing across the hallway floor
I ran up the stairs, at last.

Abigail stood and smiled at me
With her grandmother aghast,
She took me out to the balcony,
I thought that the dye was cast.
I said that I'd seen her from afar
On the balcony above,
'I want you to know I'm here to show
That I've fallen for you, in love.'

'And I've watched you from above,' she said,
'I saw the love in your eyes,
I knew that you would finally come
So it's not a great surprise.'
At this the crone had mounted the stairs,
I finally saw her smile,
She carried a platter for us to eat,
'Some sweets, will you stay awhile?'

Abigail tied them up in a cloth
To take when I left that night,
Some cherry whirls, and peppermint twirls
And chunks of Turkish Delight,
She scribbled a note that she placed within
And she'd underlined it twice,
'Whatever you do, I'm telling you,
Don't eat the Coconut Ice.'

It seems that the sweets were all home made
In the kitchen under the stair,
'My grandmother takes great pride in these,
But still, you'd better beware.'
At home I unwrapped them carefully
And I checked the Coconut Ice,
The smell was bitter like almonds so
I took Abigail's advice.

The chemist confirmed that cyanide
Was part of the recipe,
The police arrested the grandmother
And now Abigail is free.
I wish I could say she stayed with me
But she went with Raymond Bryce,
So there was a lesson learned, you see,
I never touch Coconut Ice.

Godless

He was often at the market
Signing books that no-one read,
If they had, and known the target
Then they'd not be lying dead.
For the mystic glyph inscriptions
Pointed men towards their fate,
He would say, 'You'd better read them
Or perhaps you'll be too late.'

But he seemed so insignificant
They wouldn't heed his words,
Threw his books in their collections
So they wouldn't be disturbed.
For the few who really read them
Dived right in and turned the page,
Suffered instant palpitations that
Expressed themselves in rage.

Though they didn't realise, he was
A god from outer space,
Who had come down with his minions
To save the human race,
But the human brain had limits that
Could not absorb much more,
Than the irritants that stimulate
And lead them off to war.

It came to pass that leaders heard,
Surrounded him with trucks,
And trying to suppress the word
They seized, and burned his books.

They didn't want the people having
Knowledge, at the least,
That could interfere with politics
And might burst out in peace.

The dollar ruled that ammunition,
Bombs that could be lobbed,
And hand grenades, and tank displays
They all came down to jobs.
And so they closed the market down
To end the sale of books,
That warned about conscription, and
Aspiring army cooks.

And so the god from outer space
Climbed back in his machine,
He'd tried to help the human race,
The human race was mean.
He took on board his minions
And said, 'It's getting late,'
Engaged the afterburners and
Then left us to our fate.

The Charnel House of the Plague

I sat all night in the charnel house
With a rag held over my face,
The smell down there was infernal
But I was guarding my wife's remains,
They'd picked her up in a wooden cart
When they'd cried, 'Bring out your dead,'
Thrown her on top of the corpses there
With the plague marks on her head.

I followed the cart to Winson Green
Where they tipped their load in the dark,
Down in a noisome cellar, then
They would take them out to the park,
The churchyards all were full, they said,
They'd have to dig a pit,
And bury a hundred bodies there
There was no avoiding it.

I made my way to the cellar and sat,
Holding Elizabeth's hand,
Just as she'd held my hand in life
'Til the plague swept over the land,
We'd wept together when she had felt
The swelling under her arms,
I'd vowed that I would take care of her
When freed from this life's alarms.

'You won't go into a communal pit,
I'll see that they treat you fair,'
She smiled at me on her deathbed, then
I ran my hand through her hair,

I called my brother to make the trip
To the coffinmaker he knew,
And bid him, 'Carry the casket back
Before the fever gets you!'

He came at dawn in a sorry state,
The fever was on his brow,
'The casket's out in the street,' he said,
'The coffinmaker is down.
His wife and children are dead in there,
I grabbed the one that was free,
But once you've settled Elizabeth,
You'd better get one for me.'

We dragged Elizabeth up through the grate
And rolled her into the street,
Placed her into the coffin there
Tucked in her beautiful feet,
The lid went down, such a final sound
When she finally left my life,
As we loaded her onto a horse and dray
I cried for my poor, dead wife.

They turned us away at the cemetery,
They turned us away at the church,
They wouldn't advise us where to go,
'You'll have to go off, and search.'
We came upon an abandoned house
And put her up in the eaves,
'They'll never find her,' my brother groaned
In the throes of the dread disease.

My brother died on the following day,
I left him beside the kerb,
Next to my mother and cousin Joan
They'd treated themselves with herbs,
But nothing stemmed the march of the plague
My family all but gone,
While I was immune from its deadly rays
Just me, and my father, Ron.

We walked and walked from the city square,
And sought out a country town,
We ate fresh food from the countryside
And waited the plague to go down,
I went to recover Elizabeth then,
Went back in search of my spouse,
But wandered forever the empty streets,
I couldn't remember the house!

The Dungeon

From the Minappartamento
In the middle of the night,
We walked the old Piazza
Lit by just a single light,
I could see the Madonnina
Where she overlooked Milan,
But then mia Carrenina
Shivered, so I took her hand.

We were headed for the Church
Santa Maria, in the gloom,
That held the first segreta prigione,
The torture room,
It was down below the basement
And forbidden every day,
By the Friar, Alessandro
Who kept sending us away.

Carrenina was determined
She had seen the manuscripts,
Telling of Contessa Roma
Last seen heading to its depths,
With her lover, Count Lorenzo
To be questioned there in chains
For the sins of fornication
And adultery, were the claims.

They were never seen again, and the
Franciscans would not tell,
In a secret inquisition
They sped wayward souls to hell,

But my Carrenina hungered
To complete her family tree,
It had ended there with Roma,
Rousing curiosity.

The Church door lock was ancient
And it snapped with just a twist,
So we ventured through the shadows
Found the door we'd almost missed,
Then we stepped down to the basement
Had to break two other locks,
That revealed another staircase
That was made of limestone blocks.

The air was damp and musty
There was mildew on the wall,
But the instruments of torture
Rusted there, around the hall,
There the rack and the strappado
Were like monsters from the past,
But the Judas Cradle caught the eye
Of Carrenina last.

There were awful iron cages where
The bones were still intact,
Looking hopelessly below them
As their wives and sons were racked,
But we finally turned slowly
To inspect the furthest wall,
When Carrenina cried on out;
We read, and were appalled.

The mildew scraped away to read
Lorenzo, on one stone,
Beside it, one said Roma
And the silence down there groaned,
For we knew that we had found them,
That the Franciscans had lied,
They had bricked them up behind that wall
While they were still alive.

There were hammers by the bootikens
That lay all stained in blood,
There were chisels for some torture
Staked in blocks of spattered wood,
So I seized them and attacked the wall,
'By God, we'll set them free,'
I said to Carrenina as she
Wept, and clung to me.

The mortar had turned sandy so
It powdered with each clout,
And loosened up Lorenzo's block,
I slowly edged it out,
He lay within a coffin space
His head the closest view,
But on his side, his arm thrust in,
A space they'd left them to.

One stone between their coffins
Left a hole between each space,
Enough for him to reach on through,
Hold hands, or touch her face,

But when the Roma block was moved
We saw the state of things,
Lorenzo's hand was round her throat
Still girt with ducal rings.

He'd strangled her, his mi amore,
To still her pain and fears,
When death was stalking both of them
Walled up, and she in tears,
We moved his hand to clasp on hers
Though centuries passed them by,
But as we turned to leave that place
I swear, I heard them sigh!

Wood Men

We dropped down into the forest on
A Friday afternoon,
Myself and a team of Dendronauts
Left peering through the gloom,
Our Dirigible had failed, and crashed
Right through the canopies,
We found ourselves on the forest floor,
Staring up at the trees.

There wasn't a lot of growth down there
Just dead and dying waste,
The canopy so thick, the sunlight
Couldn't penetrate.
'Now what do we do?' howled Carol Timms,
'We're eighty miles from base…'
The hole we'd punched in the canopy
Had closed, left barely a trace.

'They'll send a party out to search,'
Said Doctor Avignon,
But nobody spoke, we feared the worst,
We knew that he was wrong.
'Can somebody climb the highest tree?'
Said the pilot, Andrew Young,
The trees were a hundred and fifty feet
Where the canopy overhung.

'We'll have to walk,' said Gordon Tombs,
'We'll have to leave the ship,
We might just come on a clearing where
The trees are spread a bit,

They often fall in the monsoon rains
When the ground is waterlogged,
The roots are shallow and rip right out
Where the ground becomes a bog.'

He shouldn't have mentioned that fateful word
For the rain came teeming down,
Down in streams from the canopy
So we thought that we might be drowned,
Then with the rain there came the heat,
So humid, Carol cursed,
'We're going to sweat or drown down here,
I don't know which is worse.'

So Tombs led off with a compass that
He had, with keys on his ring,
'If we head due east we might get out,
We have to try something!'
In minutes we were soaked, and steam
Was rising from our clothes,
The mud was forming underfoot
And the smell was on the nose.

We sludged our way for an hour or two
'Til Carol Timms had cried,
'I can't go on, I'm not so strong,
My legs feel like they've died!'
Then up ahead there were cobwebs linking
Every root and tree,
And caught in the web were shrivelled bats,
How big would the spiders be?

We cut and we hacked our way through these,
They clung at every step,
But Andrew had some sort of a fit
And he couldn't catch his breath.
A spider, big as a dinner plate
Was clinging to his back,
He screamed just once, then dropped to the ground
With a fatal heart attack.

The Doctor stumbled and gashed his arm
On the bark of a giant tree,
And sap was mingling with his blood
Before he pulled it free,
Then Tombs leant back on a mildew patch
And it stung, and clung to his skin,
'I have a terrible feeling, Guys,
We'll never get out,' said Timms.

We left Andrew, and we walked on through
The web, 'til the Doctor cried,
'I feel some terrible thing is growing
Here on my arm, inside.'
We looked at the arm of Avignon
And the skin looked just like bark.
While Tombs was growing a mildew patch
Up from his hand, in the dark.

His fingers were sprouting shoots and leaves
At an ever increasing pace,
'By God, we've got to get out of here
For the sake of the human race.'

'There's things down here that shouldn't be,'
Cried Carol Timms in fear,
Then began to tear off her sodden clothes
In a fit of hysteria.

A tribe of ants ran over her skin,
Were biting her red and raw,
I beat them off as she screamed, but others
Streamed on up from the floor,
In minutes she was stripped to the bone
And sank to the ground and died,
I turned to run, with Avignon,
With Tombs ahead as a guide.

We found a spot where the trees were felled
A clearing, long and wide,
A hole was torn in the canopy
I could see a storm-lit sky,
But Avignon was sprouting leaves
And some fungal type of rot,
For then the tendrils under his feet,
Rooted him to the spot.

While Tombs was growing a fungus, green
All over his hands and face,
It grew so fast, I couldn't believe,
But I knew he'd lost his race.
It sprouted out, all over his tongue
And choked at the back of his throat,
As he fell and died, I thought he sighed,
But all that was left was his coat.

The chopper found me, dropped me a line,
I was left a gibbering wreck,
I couldn't answer their questions then,
I doubt I could answer them yet!
I'd seen men basically turned to wood,
I'd seen one turn to a tree,
So didn't know whether I'd dare to show
The fungus that's growing on me!

Eternal Youth

I was travelling through a countryside
That I'd never seen before,
As it grew dark, the mountainsides
Loomed threatening, over my car,
The cloud hung low in a louring sky
And my headlights cut through the gloom,
Ahead on the twisting, bending road
I had hopes of a cosy room.

There wasn't a house or a farm out there,
The valley was threading down,
The deeper it went, the darker yet
With still no sign of a town,
I thought that I'd have to drive all night
And my eyes were growing dim,
When back in the trees, I saw a light
And a sign: 'The Dew Drop Inn'.

I pulled at the bell for the Publican
And I heard a shuffle inside,
A shadow loomed, and the hinges creaked
And the door swung open wide,

A man so gaunt that his face was grey
And his sallow cheeks were thin,
Stood trembling in the doorway there
In the hall of the Dew Drop Inn!'

I followed him in, not saying a word,
He motioned me into the bar,
Then poured me a whiskey and water
While I stared at a glass topped jar,
It drew my gaze as I sipped my drink
For the contents bubbled and swirled,
And I said: 'Just where is the Dew Drop Inn?'
He replied: 'At the End of the World!'

His voice came bubbling out of his chest
Like the rasp of a rusty saw,
His hands were trembling, where they lay
And he kept his eyes on the door.
'That jar, it changes its colours, look!
From red, through green and gold...'
He said: 'They told me one sip from that
And a man would never grow old!'

I stared at him, and I saw him frown
With a tear at the edge of his eye,
This ancient man with the trembling hand
And I said: 'Well, that was a lie!'
He shook his head and he turned to me
'It depends what you want it for,
I was twenty-two when I took my sip...
I'm a hundred and sixty four!'

'I didn't age for a hundred years
I revelled in youth, so long,
But suddenly I grew weary, thought
That there must have been something wrong!
I lost the zest for a youthful life,
Was beginning to feel my years,
All of my friends were dead and gone,
This life is a valley of tears!'

'You're telling me that one sip from this
Will give me a hundred - True?
I'll still be fit and I'll still be strong,
At a hundred and thirty two?'
'You will, but there's a condition
You must take on the Dew Drop Inn,
And stay in this cursèd valley then
'Til a seeker of youth walks in!'

I'm standing behind the counter with
My eyes on the outer door,
I've stood like stone for forty years
And paced a track on the floor,
The Publican left, the moment I sipped
He went with a joyous cry,
In search of a path from the Dew Drop Inn
Where at last, he could finally die!

The Sound of the Spheres

The Rastenberg Philharmonic had sat,
Were shuffling in their seats,
And tuning their various instruments
To play '*The Survivor Suite*'.
It had only been played just once before,
They knew they were taking a chance,
The conductor and several cellists had gone
Right after *Svrili's Dance*!

One moment, the baton was waved in the air,
The next, the podium was clear,
A cellist had sawed at an awful E flat
Before he had disappeared;
Then holes had appeared in the group at the front
Where cellists and violins sat,
And all that was left of the treble bassoon
Was a sandwich, under his hat.

It wasn't as if they hadn't been warned
For Borchnik appeared on the stage,
'I scribbled this suite in a white hot heat
As I paced, in a boiling rage!
For those sitting close to the glockenspiel,
They really should cover their ears,
For once that crescendo of flute, lute and cello
Is heard - that's the Sound of the Spheres!'

Karamov turned to the audience, bowed,
Then tapped with his baton, twice,
He wouldn't be fazed to the end of his days
Though the Devil was tumbling the dice!

He looked at the fear-crazed Orchestra
Who'd heard about Borchnik's curse,
Then launched them in to *The Wages of Sin*
As an introductory verse!

The music was nothing like you would expect,
It capered and trilled, and it soared,
It spoke of the aeons of military might,
Of the soldier that fell on his sword,
The audience sat with their open jaws
As it thrilled and it burst into flight,
And carried them out where the planets sang
In a paean to endless night!

The music it raged, and the music roared
And it came to *Svrili's Dance*,
A blonde violinist took off for the door,
No way was she taking a chance!
A hole opened over a cellist's head
And swallowed the glockenspiel,
While Karamov's face went as white as the dead
When he found himself out in a field!

The Orchestra, crazed, seemed unable to stop,
The instruments sang in their hands,
The audience freaked as the piccolo peaked
And the harpsichord melted in strands,
They made for the exits in panic and fear
For the horror that waited outside,
A mammoth was leaning against the front door,
And a raptor was caught in mid-stride.

It took seven weeks for the madness to stop,
And Borchnik was run out of town,
While Karamov wanders where dinosaurs crop,
Conducting some thoughts of his own.
The Rastenberg Orchestra's now in recess,
Unlikely to play now for years,
The musicians agree that there isn't a fee
That would bring back *The Sound of the Spheres!*

The Cavalier

He'd wandered into the party through
The French Doors, facing the lake,
Was vague, and missing a bob or two,
Perhaps he'd made a mistake?
Taken a left at the crossroads where
The kids had hidden the sign,
Instead of a right to the Graham's house,
I'd ask him, given the time.

The party was getting out of hand
The punch was spiked with gin,
And vodka and tequila and…
God knows what else was in!
For Jane was down to her underwear
While Pat fell down in a heap,
And Margaret danced on the table while
Her kids were sound asleep.

The clock in the hall struck midnight then
And I was getting tired,
I went on the hunt for Carolyn,
I thought that she'd expired,

But there she was, in the corner with
The stranger in the hat,
A funny thing with a feather in
And fancy dress, at that.

I thought that I'd introduce myself,
I'd not seen him before,
Perhaps he worked at the agency,
I'd ask, she'd know the score,
But Carolyn acted nervous when
I tried to hold her hand,
'What gentleman is this, I pray?'
He asked of Carolyn.

'Oh Phil, he's simply a husband,'
She replied, she was sublime,
I note she mentioned 'a husband' but
No mention that 'He's mine!'
'And what are these folk that prate, disport
And act themselves remiss,
Is he from the Long Parliament?
God help him, if he is!'

I knew the punch had been tampered with
But he hadn't been there long,
Maybe he'd savoured something else,
Who knew what he was on!
But Carolyn gave me that funny look
And I edged back into the room,
Leaving the two of them talking there
In the corner, in the gloom.

We'd always had an arrangement, she
Had friends, and I had mine,
We never questioned each other, and
We found that it worked out fine,
She'd spend a night on the town or so
And fix me up a tray,
While I'd go visiting Annabel
For a tumble in the hay.

We'd purchased the house at Kineton,
When she'd said: 'It has such charm!'
And I was content to be out there
In the country, near a farm,
They said the place was historic
Dating back to the civil war,
But not 'til the night of the party
Did I give it a second thought.

By one, the following morning, when
The party was winding down,
I found that Carolyn disappeared
With the stranger to the town,
She sent me a mobile message, 'Will
You come and get me, Phil?
I'm right in the heart of a skirmish
Down the slope, just by Edgehill!'

I drove to the ancient battlefield
In the dark, on a Moonless night,
But nothing stirred in the field out there
In the beam of the car's headlight,

My phone lit up with another call
And her voice came drifting through,
'My God, I'm stuck in a battle, Phil,
In 1642!'

She'd taken off with the Cavalier,
I knew what he was by now,
A straggler caught in the folds of time
That had fetched up here, somehow,
And Carolyn faded into the past
As she'd made it more than clear,
I'm the only man with a wife that ran
Away with a Cavalier!

Daydreams

I sit every day in an office, and play
With a ledger that carries my name,
And stare from the window, the clouds scudding grey
On a sky that is always the same,
The river winds down by the weed-winding bank
But is sluggish and slow in its ride,
Heading on out to the estuary, carrying
Debris, adrift on the tide.

Just about here was the place, where in fear
They once straddled the river in chains,
And called up the hundreds, with helmet and shield
To defend this poor land from the Danes,
And often I peer through the rain and the mist
And the grime on the window without,
Imagining Vikings enmeshed in the chains,
And struggling there, to get out.

The office is staffed by grey people in need
Who would like to get home to the wife,
They mutter in tones of their essence and creed
While some of us just want a life,
But Caroline Chambers is not one of these
She's a flower, sprung out of the weeds,
And I see, as she flits between coffees and teas
She's a Saxon, her coffee is mead.

She pushes the trolley that carries the swords
And the helmets, and buckler's too,
As she stands by my desk for a chat and a rest
She's defiant; she's one of the few.

As she stares out the window, I hear her declare
That she's not going to put up with this,
The Danish accountant has stolen her chair
And her venom is mouthed with a hiss.

'I'll poison his coffee, you see if I don't,'
And her Saxon blood comes to the boil,
I get fleeting visions of lopping his head,
Or perhaps we should boil him in oil?
She wanders away and she hands out the pay
As I ravish her there in my mind,
And she stares up at me from a puddle of tea
Mutters, 'How could you be so unkind?'

The following day I can see the affray
As the Legions march into the town,
The Roman Centurions glitter with gold
With their standards held high, not put down,
And Caroline Chambers, Welsh bonnet and dress
With a lilt in her voice, brings the teas,
She stands by the chariot of Boadicea,
Brings the Legions of Rome to their knees!

I sit every day in an office, and play
With a ledger that carries my name,
And stare from the window, the clouds scudding grey
On a sky that is always the same,
But Caroline Chambers has shared in my dreams
Though she has no idea, she's my wife,
As I live in the daydreams of coloured and grey dreams
And desperately search for a life!

1400

I've devoted my life to poetry
Whenever I've had the time,
Created whole towns and villages
And even the people rhyme.
There's only supposed to be six plots
In the stories we have to tell,
And half of them aim for heaven, while
The rest of them end in hell.

But I've written fourteen hundred tales
And each of them has a plot,
With climaxes in the middle, and
A twist in the tail, or not.
There's anger, love and revenge in there
Mixed in the poetic stew,
And some of the plots are quite threadbare,
But they're all written for you.

My women are all quite beautiful,
My men are as hard as nails,
They constantly search for love, I find,
In all of my paper trails.
But most have an itch they have to scratch,
For some of them there's regret,
They pay the cost when a lover's lost
And it haunts their stories yet.

I often scribble in witches, ghouls,
And spirits that have no souls,
That hover around the edges, with
Their indeterminate goals.

I look to the distant future now
For tales you'll never forget,
And trust to fate that it's not too late
For a million stories yet.